The divine poet through his gift of *Tirukural* gives maxims to serve as guidance for all classes, sections, denominations, etc., in the world. *Tirukural* couplets have the added significance of providing invaluable advice for all times, as it takes into consideration the wider aspects, with necessary changes, of human nature beyond national, religious and linguistic boundaries. *Tirukural* gives added value because the author, Tiruvalluvar, had the rare distinction of having lived the ideal life as portrayed in his immortal work. *Tirukural* shows a way of life applicable to all sections of society, from kings and nobles down to the common man. This teaching echoes the sentiments expressed in many other religious texts, such as *Tirumantiram, Naladiyar, Saiva Tirumuraigal* of the Nayanars and *Vaishnava Prapanthams* of the Alwars. ¶Good conduct with abiding moral values and sincere brotherhood are the centerpieces of Tiruvalluvar's teachings. Kindness to fellow human beings, full sense of humanity and human values will ensure a better world, according to the tenets of *Tirukural.* In a world full of turmoil, the *Tirukural* stands as a beacon to a peaceful way of life, and this coupled with the daily recitation of the Panchakshara Mantra, "Namasivaya," found at the heart of the *Vedas*, will ensure peace and well being.

Dr. T.S. Sambamurthy Sivachariar, Head of the South India Archaka Sangam; Head Priest, Shree Kalikambal Kovil; Chennai, Tamil Nadu, India

The *Tirukural* was very dear to Satguru Siva Yogaswami of Jaffna. Under his holy feet I have been brought up as one of his devotees from my early age of eight years. Whenever I visited, he spoke to me, directed and blessed me always through the sacred *Kural*. In 1949, Satguru Sivaya Subramuniyaswami made a vow to bring together the best of both the East and the West. In 1999, with his latest book, *Weaver's Wisdom*, he has successfully brought this to the West. Referring to the statue of Saint Tiruvalluvar at Kanya Kumari, Subramuniyaswami states, "While America's Statue of Liberty is a metal monument to political freedom and social promise, Tiruvalluvar stands as a stone statement of political wisdom, social duty and the spiritual promise of *dharma*." ¶We should not confine Tiruvalluvar only to Tamil Nadu. He belongs to the world. *Weaver's Wisdom* is beyond race, religion and nationality. It will enrich the life of a person as he or she journeys along this Eternal Path. The wisdom of the weaver is a vital part of our lives, and it will pave the way for success in life.

Tiru A. Kandiah, Ph.D.; Author of *Malarum Manamum*; Former Head, Department of Tamil, University of Kelaniya, Sri Lanka; Former Professor, University of London; Sydney, Australia

Weaver's Wisdom

திருக்குறள்
நெசவாளியின் ஞானம்

First Edition

Copyright © 1999
by Satguru Sivaya Subramuniyaswami

Weaver's Wisdom is published by Himalayan Academy. All rights reserved. Lovingly designed and typeset by the *acharyas* and swamis of the Saiva Siddhanta Yoga Order, 107 Kaholalele Road, Kapaa, Hawaii 96746-9304 USA.

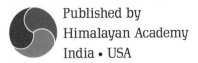

Published by
Himalayan Academy
India • USA   PRINTED IN USA

Library of Congress Catalog Card Number 99-071795
ISBN 0-945497-76-9

www.hindu.org/ashram/

Weaver's Wisdom

Ancient Precepts for
A Perfect Life

திருக்குறள்

நெசவாளியின் ஞானம்

An American English translation of
Saint Tiruvalluvar's ancient *Tirukural*

Satguru Sivaya Subramuniyaswami

Indra Sharma
1999

Dedication

Samarpanam

சமர்ப்பணம்

THIS DEDICATION IS THREE-FOLD: FIRST TO HONOR MY SATGURU, SIVA YOGASWAMI, THE LAUDED AND PROCLAIMED PONTIFF OF THE THREE MILLION JAFFNA Tamil peoples, the 161st successor in the esteemed line of the Nandinatha Sampradaya's Kailasa Parampara, and to Tiru Mylvaganam, whom Yogaswami requested to squeeze grapes into juice for me with his own hands while I sat facing the devotees at the *satguru's* left side in 1949. Mylvaganam was also present at the opening of the Sri Subramuniya Ashram in Alaveddy in the early 70s, and years later at the opening of the Subramuniya Kottam in Kopay, where he lives today. In recent years, despite the terrible conflicts in his country, this great man has been translating the *Tirukural* from our English verses into modern Tamil for the next generation. Long ago, Yogaswami gave a *sadhana* to him to memorize *Tirukural* and to recite some of the verses daily. Humorously, the youthful, Oxford-educated Mylvaganam said, "Swami, what if I forget some days?" Yogaswami said, "Then I will come as a centipede and bite you." Mylvaganam has testified now, at 90 years of age, that he has been bitten forty times or more, always soon after he had neglected to recite the verses. He said, "I now see that Yogaswami was preparing me to translate for Gurudeva into modern Tamil all the verses I memorized so many years ago." We also dedicate this book to Justice of Peace Tiru S. Subramaniam, who witnessed Satguru Yogaswami's giving me a slap on the back as I was leaving the gate to his compound one morning by which he transferred his *samskaras*, or vital divine spiritual energies.

Contents

Porulatakkam
பொருளடக்கம்

PART ONE: ON VIRTUE

Section I: Prologue

Section II: The Way of the Householder

Introduction

Arimukam

அறிமுகம்

M ANY YEARS AGO WHEN I WAS FIRST IN SRI LAN-
KA—THAT WAS IN 1949—I MADE A VOW TO BRING
TOGETHER THE BEST OF THE EAST AND THE BEST
of the West. Living with a traditional Saivite family that in-
formally adopted me in those early days, I was introduced to
the *Tirukural*. I found it to be one of the most important scriptures in all of Asia, so enchanting and so very practical. It
contains wondrously no-nonsense insights on life, teaching us
how to deal with the various feelings and circumstances that
we encounter in our internal life and our interactions with
others. In this sense, the *Tirukural* is the most accessible and
relevant sacred text I know, applying to everyday matters and
common concerns.

The *Tirukural* is a 2,200-year-old South Indian Dravidian
classic on ethical living. Not unaware that there are advo-
cates of later dates (from ca 200 bce down to ca 400 ce) we
honor here the prevalent Tamil tradition. Its 1,330 verses were
written by a Tamil weaver sage named Tiruvalluvar. I have
named his work *Weaver's Wisdom*. It is called *Tirukural* in
the Tamil language. *Tiru* means "holy" or "sacred," and *kural*
describes a brief verse or literary couplet.

The poetic masterpiece you are holding in your hands is
one of the most revered scriptures in South India, where
every child learns to recite its verses by heart. Hindus there
regard it with the same reverence that Buddhists regard the
Buddha's *Dhammapada* and Christians regard Jesus' "Sermon
on the Mount." In fact, other religions also claim it as their
own. The Jains proclaim it theirs, saying it expresses precisely

their ideals of nonviolence, of *dharma*, of asceticism, vegetarianism and other aspects of Jainism. The Christians have argued that the *Tirukural* is so profound and filled with such compassion that it must have been influenced by the Christian missionaries who, their legends say, came to South India in the first century CE (300 years after native historians assert it was written). Many are surprised to find that the *Tirukural* is still sworn upon in the courts of law in South India's state of Tamil Nadu, just as the Christian *Bible* and Muslim *Koran* are sworn on elsewhere. Just as the Sikhs worship their holy text, *Adi Granth,* devout Hindus venerate with a sacred ceremony, called *puja,* the weaver's scripture in temples and home shrines. Albert Schweitzer, medical missionary and Christian theologian in Africa, considered it one of the grandest achievements of the human mind, writing, "Like the Buddha and the *Bhagavad Gita,* the *Kural* desires inner freedom from the world and a mind free from hatred. You find the quintessence of the best gems of thoughts in the *Kural,* a living ethic of love and liberation." Indeed, many claim that the *Tirukural* is man's earliest statement of the ostensibly contemporary ecumenical tenets, for it is free of the dogmatic bias that commonly attends religious scriptures. The Father of modern India, Mahatma Gandhi, took to these verses in his own spiritual life, telling his people, "Only a few of us know the name of Tiruvalluvar. The North Indians do not know the name of the great saint. There is none who has given such a treasure of wisdom like him."

One of the hallmarks of Saint Tiruvalluvar's genius was his ability to deftly define and subtly delineate Sanatana Dharma, the Eternal Spiritual Path, to all men equally, never limiting his audience to a sectarian view. Even when he speaks directly of God, Whom he addresses as *Adi Bhagavan, Iraivan* and *Kadavul*—ancient Tamil words for Supreme God Siva—the weaver's broad heart praises not the God of this faith or that, but sings his panegyric to "God Primordial," "the Incomparable One," "the Gracious One" or "the Compassionate One." In other words, everyone's God.

Having honored the Worshipful One, the weaver then praises rain, for without rain's gift of life all the human experience would be impossible. The third chapter speaks of renunciation, *sannyasa*, for to him the renunciate monk is the most noble exemplar of humanity, the highest of souls, the minister of Sanatana Dharma, nowadays called Hinduism in English, Indu Samayam in Tamil, Hindutva in Sanskrit, Hindouisme in French, Hinduismo in Spanish, Religione Hindú in Italian, and Hinduismus in German. He exalts renunciation as a way of life opposed to that of the householder, encouraging ardent souls seeking the realization of their own True Being, to take up their faith with vigor and to live the detached, selfless life of a renunciate—noninvolvement in the joys and sorrows of the world, which he also describes in minute detail in other chapters. Without giving us a hint of what he is up to, the weaver has thus defined in his first three chapters the three fundamental dimensions of Saiva Siddhanta philosophy— God, world and soul, known in Tamil as Pati, *pasam* and *pasu*. It is indicative of his subtle literary style that Tiruvalluvar begins the very first verse with the first letter of the Tamil alphabet, "A," and ends the last line of verse 1,330 with the final letter, "N," quietly informing us that he has covered all human concerns, from A to Z.

In Tamil literature, *kural* names the very difficult and disciplined *venpa* meter in which the verses were written. Each verse is extremely short, containing only two lines of seven measures. In fact, it is the shortest form of stanza in the Tamil language. In many ways these couplets are similar to the Sanskrit *shloka*. The scripture consists of 133 chapters with each chapter elucidating a different aspect of human virtue or human fault. There are ten couplets per chapter, making a total of 1,330 couplets.

Although it has been translated into English by many scholars, the *Tirukural* has never been widely known in the Western world. There is a similar work, written in modern times by the Syrian-born American mystic Kahlil Gibran (1883-1931), called *The Prophet*, which has become a beloved classic. Everyone knows and loves this masterful work. *The Prophet* parallels the *Tirukural* in many ways. Both books speak in profound yet understandable terms of love and friendship, of health and death, of joy and sorrow. It is our hope that the *Tirukural—Weaver's Wisdom*—will find its place beside *The Prophet* and be known by the wider world as the gem that it is, showing how the Tamil Saivites have, to this very day, maintained their heritage, rich culture and religious fervor.

In the many days to come, the world will acknowledge this great people and their lofty culture, a way of life nurtured in the womb of Saiva Samayam, Saivite Hinduism, the resilient religion that has stood the test of time, that has survived invasions by alien cultures, faiths and imposed systems of law and government, that has survived efforts from outsiders to infiltrate, dilute and destroy their religion, culture and language, that has survived poverty, over-population and modernization. It is a faith that lives as proudly and profoundly today as it did perhaps ten thousand years ago. What other culture can make such a claim?

Much of what the weaver writes revolves around the home, which resonates well with today's calls to return to traditional family values. He speaks of the faithful husband and the devoted wife, of the upright children they raise and the joys they experience, of the value of relationship and how to nurture and sustain it. He speaks of age and its merits, of the importance of honoring the elderly, of caring for and not abandoning them.

Nor is the weaver a stranger to difficult issues that still perplex us. He speaks of killing and of the king's duty to execute murderers. He speaks of alcohol addiction, of the debilitating effects of gambling, of adultery and the tragic loss of a life lived in poverty or lazy indifference. He guides us in matters of education, and warns against the life-sapping effect of lack of knowledge. He speaks of a strong military, of spies and of advisors with personal agendas, of fools and their ways and wastes. He knows of the wiles of real enemies and has much to tell modern man about overcoming opposition, about being wise against antagonists' crafty ways and thus surviving the attacks of foes. He speaks of making money and of how money is squandered and lost. He explores purity, kindness, humility, right thought, right action, friendship and all forms of virtuous living, and he boldly offers stern warning as to the consequence of base, sinful thoughts and actions. With great force, he decries the agonies caused by meat-eating and commends traditional Hindu vegetarianism. All along the way we encounter his humor, which he uses to great effect and which makes us laugh even as it points to our most stubborn flaws and comic foibles.

Hinduism's four legitimate goals of human life are *dharma, artha, kama* and *moksha,* known in English as virtue, wealth, love and liberation. In the *Tirukural,* Saint Tiruvalluvar spoke in depth on the first three. Under the heading of virtue, he discusses the ways of the householder and the monk, focusing on good conduct and its opposite. In the chapters on wealth he speaks of business, government, politics and the building of the nation. In the final twenty-five chapters on love (not included in this edition), he discusses the relationships of men and women. Valluvar also discussed the fourth and final goal of life, liberation from rebirth, especially in the chapters on the way of the renunciate. As the four *Vedas* outline the path to salvation by delineation of the destination, the *Tirukural* carefully explains how to live while treading the path to that ultimate goal. Along with the *Tirumantiram* (composed by the great Tamil mystic, Rishi Tirumular, during the same period) which explains the means to Self Realization, spiritual *yogas* and liberation, these two classics form a complete whole, covering *dharma, artha, kama* and *moksha.*

The *Tirukural* is Tiruvalluvar's only known work; and though it is relatively short compared to such sacred texts as the *Dhammapada* or the *Adi Granth,* it was sufficient to bring renown to a simple and highly observant weaver, making him a venerated sage and lawgiver of the ancient Tamil Dravidian people. The *Kural's* relative brevity is also its strength, as is its immense practicality. Here is no esoteric doctrine, no other-worldly speculation, but adages for practical daily life in every age, for mankind does not change all that much from era to era. It is my hope and aspiration that this masterpiece finds its way into your heart.

In his work, Tiruvalluvar chose a topic—such as children, friendship or avoidance of anger—and gave us ten different couplets on the one subject. To properly understand his perspective, all ten couplets must be read, for they are like facets of a gem—each reflecting the light of his understanding slightly differently, and the richness of his comprehension. Not infrequently, the subject of one chapter's last verse will serve as the transition to the next chapter's first, like one thread tied to another to continue the weaving. In the opening few verses he tends to focus on the subject at hand, while moving in the latter verses into more specific matters and admonishing against failure to apply noble ideals found in the verses above. In other words, he gets tougher as the verses progress down the page.

It has been explained to us that the saint spent the fullness of his life quietly observing, simply observing, the human condition. Then, toward the end of his life, he was asked to speak out and share the wisdom others in the community knew he possessed. This book, comprising 108 chapters, was his response. I hope you will allow Saint Tiruvalluvar's insights to spark your own intuition and reveal from within yourself the laws which he, too, discovered within himself. Do not look upon this scripture as something "out there." Meditation and reflection will reveal that its knowledge lies within, vibrantly alive and dynamically real. It is impossible not to be moved by the broad compassion and the direct discernment of this holy man. Let him enrich your life as you journey along this Eternal Path, the Sanatana Dharma.

Alas, in Bharat yesterday and in the days of Tiruvalluvar, the art of weaving was a low-caste occupation. Valluvar was a member of a trade group, *jati,* certainly not accepted into the social circles of the higher castes. Still, the weavers' cloth was used extensively by the *brahmins* (the priestly caste), and the *kshatriyas* (the governing class), to adorn their bodies, and by, the *vaishyas* (the merchant caste), in bartering with other merchants. Yes, weavers were near the bottom of the social scale in India then, as today. It is interesting to note that this man who lived low in the social structure left a legacy that makes all Tamils proud, that shines among human endeavors, and outshines virtually every high-caste neighbor he had.

Stories of the Ideal Wife, Vasuki

Saint Tiruvalluvar lived with his wife, Vasuki, in what is today a part of Chennai in South India. Vasuki was the perfect example of simple devotion and traditional intelligent cooperation with her husband, and several stories, handed down in the oral tradition from generation to generation, are told depicting the marvel of the harmony in their marriage. We cannot know for certain that these stories contain only the

facts of those days long ago, but they do show us what Tamil village life was like two thousand years ago and what was considered to be the ideal home and the ideal householder.

Legends say that Vasuki was the daughter of Margasahayam, an affluent farmer of the region who was impressed with Valluvar's right living and lofty thinking and proposed his young daughter's hand in marriage. When the proposal was brought to Valluvar, he agreed, provided his betrothed passed a small test. Tests were common in his culture—a man testing his prospective wife, a guru testing a candidate for initiation, a common man testing a friend before opening his heart and home. When they first met, Valluvar made this request to Vasuki: to take a handful of sand and boil it into rice for him. The girl took the sand without the slightest resistance and, in perfect faith that this holy person's wishes would manifest, proceeded to prepare the requested meal. Miraculously, the sand turned to savory rice, which she served her husband-to-be. Right then, it is said, the poet took Vasuki to be his wife.

As the marriage grew stronger and deeper, villagers began to admire the relationship. Many would come to Valluvar to ask his opinion about marriage, about household life, about the relationships between men and women. On one occasion a neighbor came to the weaver's home and asked, "Some say the path of the ascetic monk is the highest. Others say no, it is that of the householder which holds most merit. What do you think?" Without giving a direct answer to the query, Valluvar invited the man to stay a few days in his home as a guest. A few mornings later Vasuki was drawing water at the family well just outside. Such wells, called *kineru*, are made so that a long wooden pole holds at one end a wooden bucket suspended on a long rope and at the other a counterweight of stones. The empty bucket is let down to the water in the open well and then the counterweight helps lift the water to the top. As the bucket reached above the above-ground level, Vasuki's husband loudly called for her to come to his side. She came instantly, abandoning the task and rushing to her beloved. The guest was astonished, not only at her responsiveness, but at a small miracle he had witnessed. As the story goes, when Vasuki left the well at once at her husband's calling, the bucket was in mid air, filled with water. Instead of falling back into the well, it remained suspended in the same position, apparently defying the law of gravity, until she returned to her wifely chore.

On another morning, Valluvar and his guest were seated together for breakfast, which consisted of plain cold rice from the day before. This was a typical South Indian breakfast, since there was no refrigeration to keep food. Frugality was an important discipline for survival. Suddenly, the weaver said to his wife, "This rice is too hot to eat. It is burning my fingers!" Vasuki swiftly grabbed a fan and began fanning the cold rice, which had been served on a banana leaf. Wonder of wonders, steam rose from the rice as she sought to cool it.

On yet another day as Valluvar was diligently plying his handloom, he accidentally dropped a shuttle to the floor. Though it was midday and the sun shone brightly, the weaver, apparently deep in thought, called to his wife to bring a lamp so he might look for the lost shuttle. Vasuki quickly lit the oil lamp and brought it to her husband without the slightest consciousness of the unreasonableness of her husband's request.

The guest left the home soon thereafter, having witnessed all this. No direct answer was ever given to the original question, but the moral of the story is that the visitor had seen with his own eyes a most marvelous marriage partnership and learned Valluvar's unspoken message, that a man whose wife is equal to Vasuki would best follow the householder path, though without such a wife the ascetic's path is preferred: "If a man masters the duties of married life, what further merits could monkhood offer him?"

Valluvar and Vasuki lived a peaceful, loving life, and apparently had children to delight them and family in great numbers to offer support and affection in their later years. As Vasuki was about to die, her husband asked if there was anything he could do for her. "Yes, dear husband," came her faint reply. "All our wedded life I have had a question which you could answer. From the first day of our marriage, I have been placing a small cup of fresh water and a needle beside you at every meal. May I know, my Lord, why you bid me to do this?"

Valluvar replied, "Dearest wife, I wanted the water and needle nearby so that, if you spilled any rice while serving me, I would be able to pick it up with the needle and rinse it with the water. However, as you never dropped a single grain in all those years, there was never an occasion to put these things to use." Her question answered, Vasuki breathed her last. The story idealizes the wifely attitude of never questioning her husband, and shows how perfectly Vasuki carried out her duties, not once in all their life dropping so much as a single grain of rice!

Valluvar cremated Vasuki as tradition dictated, then returned home to write a poem to her: "O, my beloved, who is sweeter than my daily food. O my darling, who has never once disobeyed me. O gentle one, who rubbing my feet, would go to bed after me and rise before, are you gone? How can slumber ever come again to my unslumbering eyes?"

The Tamil understanding of the husband-and-wife relationship is vastly different from modern thinking, which stresses sameness and equality. Yet, those who have seen the deepness of such a family and such a marriage would never call it antiquated. The Tamil wife is pure in thought, devoted to her duties, perfect in hospitality to guests. She is frugal, strong and modest, never bold. She adores her husband and never even looks into the eyes of another man. She is, they say, the authoress of her husband's renown and glory, the support that lifts him high in the eyes of others. These sentiments are exactly reflected in the Jewish tradition, which recommends that husbands read Proverbs 31 to their wives during domestic religious ceremonies.

Consider the words of Tiru M. Arunachalam of Jaffna, Sri Lanka, a noted historian and philosopher: "The Hindu dharma enjoins the dutiful wife to worship her husband as God Himself. A woman who observes this code in life earns for herself the name of *pati-vrata* (which means 'Godly vow taker'). Our ancient *Epics* and *Puranas* abound in the stories of such dutiful wives. Savitri, Anushya, Arundati are a few. Chief among such wives famous among the Tamils and in literary tradition is Vasuki."

To this very day Vasuki is the role model of tens of millions of Tamil women who pray to Lord Siva that their lives may be as loving and virtuous as this remarkably unspoiled lady's. Differing from their northern counterparts, the Tamils have rejected verses and advice in the *Mahabharata* and *Ramayana* that are said to diminish womankind. For the Tamils it is not Rama's wife Sita but Vasuki, the weaver's wife, who is the incomparable woman, the ideal partner, the noblest lady—as is Parvati to Siva.

The Weaver's Place in History

We are now going into the long, long ago, thousands of years back in human history, when the nations of India, then called Bharat, were already quite advanced and well organized and the culture had, in all that really matters, reached a sophistication that even today is hard to equal. The Sanatana Dharma was already a highly sophisticated religion, and the people were well-balanced and abundant spiritually, socially, culturally, educationally and economically.

India had already enjoyed a long history. Archeology tells us that stone tools and hand axes found in the North show human presence in 500,000 BCE, and in Tamil Nadu, in the South, in 470,000 BCE. According to the earliest dating theories, the great Vedic era in Bharat (the Hindus' name for India) had begun after the last ice age, fully 12,000 years ago, and by 9,000 years ago the Indus-Sarasvati Valley civilization was growing grains, worshiping the Gods and building elaborate cities with sun-baked mud bricks. As the millennia passed, the *Vedas* evolved, temples were built, and languages emerged, all long before the Pyramids of Egypt were even started. Historians say that weaving of fabrics was widespread in India 5,000 years ago. Weaving was honored recently in *Newsweek* magazine as one of the hundred greatest inventions of the human mind, one which allowed the human race to migrate to all parts of the planet. The tradition says that by 1915 BCE the Sangam Period began in Tamil Nadu, when sages and pandits explored the subtle arts and sciences, the philosophies and yogas. Thus, all this would have happened before the time of the *Mahabharata*, before Moses led the Jewish people out of Egypt, before the Trojan War in Greece and before the Roman Empire was inaugurated by Julius Caesar.

It was in the South of India, among the Tamil-speaking peoples, that a culture surpassed by few others grew through the centuries and finally produced a wonderfully insightful weaver named Tiruvalluvar. During the time the couplets in this book were scribed, two centuries before Christ, the Great Wall of China was being built and Buddhism in India was in the ascendant. King Ashoka's famed reign had just ended and the great Chola Empire of Tamil Nadu, where the weaver lived, was just beginning its thousand-year rule. As G. Ravindran Nair writes: "Tiruvalluvar lived during a period when the Chera, Chola and Pandya kings were ruling over different parts of Tamil Nadu, with their overseas contacts with countries ranging from Egypt, Greece and Rome in the West; Burma, Malaya, Singapore and China in the East; Ceylon in the South and the Himalayan kingdoms in the North."

The remarkable government of the Chola Empire stretched the length and breadth of South India, throughout Sri Lanka into Malaysia and into the rest of Asia, ruled around the year 1000 by Rajaraja Chola, after whom the empire was named. Saint Auvaiyar, the great mystical *yogini* and Ganesha *bhaktar*, lived, some say, at the very time of Tiruvalluvar. Historians have even thought they were brother and sister. Patanjali, author of the *Yoga Sutras*, may also have been a contemporary of the author of this book, along with Maharishi Nandinatha and his disciple, Rishi Tirumular, author of the *Tirumantiram*. In fact, while North India was still reeling from the failed invasions of Greece's Alexander the Great, in South India, yoga, art, music and literature were as advanced as anyplace on Earth. Tamil Nadu was then a nation, separate in its language and politics. It had its king and ministers, its navy and army, and it had reached through trade other nations in Southeast Asia. It was a proud time for the Tamil people, among the most civilized cultures anywhere.

Now that we know where we are in time, shall we now learn where we are in philosophy, religion, proficiency and protocol? It was here in this blessed land that the ancient Dravidians thrived, a Caucasian people of dark skin. It was here that the religion was the worship and realization of Siva, the Supreme One, the immanent and transcendent Lord, neither male nor female but both, timeless, formless, spaceless, yet pervading the universe. Siva's Holy Feet were worshiped in abandon in temples that stand today as monuments of a living past which is now a living present. Born of no one, beholden to no one, the Supreme Creator of all the 330 million Gods and trillions of *devas*, as well as embodied souls, is honored and praised today in these golden-domed, fifty-acre-and-more magnificent temples, such as Madurai and Chidambaram, built in an era whose splendor has not yet been surpassed.

In every *yuga*, or era, there are instinctive, intellectual and superconscious people in different ratios. These the weaver calls base men, learned men and perfect or knowing men. Instinctive people are those guided by their emotions. Typically, they are the builders and farmers, the craftsmen and servants. They live by the sweat of their brow, and their honest physical labor is the bedrock of society. They react quickly and impulsively and are mainly prompted by fear, chiefly motivated by greed. They worry, have many doubts, and mistrust even those with good intentions. The crudest among them assault with fists and beat the flesh of others, even their own dear children and beloved spouse.

The intellectuals are dependent upon the opinions of others, right or wrong. They are the treasury of accumulated knowledge, the teachers and analyzers, the businessmen, planners and administrators, the bedrock of science, government and intellectual endeavor. They look to the past for solutions to the problems in the present, and usually don't see far into the future. The crudest among them are argumentative and have a conceited opinion of themselves hardly equaled by others. They make up their own rules, not worrying overmuch about laws, community or tradition, and readily challenge any and all prevailing beliefs and systems. They lash out with words and emotions, and hurt the minds and sometimes irreparably disturb the emotions of others, even their cherished offspring and wedded spouse.

The superconscious, or intuitive, men and women depend on their intellect as a tool to record their insights and far-seeing premonitions. They depend on their abilities of reason to check their intuitions, knowing that intuition sees before thinking about what has been seen. They know that intuition is above reason but never conflicts with reason. These are the priests, the rishis, the yogis and gurus, the behind-the-scenes guides of the lawmakers and ratifiers of their plans. They are the heralds of creativity and the defenders of the faith. They hold to the laws, follow divine direction, dharma, and always listen inwardly for proper timing to advise others in the implementation of plans. These mature souls live by the divine law of *ahimsa*, not hurting others physically, emotionally or mentally. They are the exemplars in each *yuga*, millennium, century or decade and arise among and from the instinctives and the intellectuals, lifted by their *sadhanas*, their penance and their purity. Their example gives abundant hope for everyone in a community to rise as they did.

The story is told in India of the beautiful lotus flower that arises out of the mud. Its roots tangle below, as do instinctive people. Its stem is long and proud, reaching for the sky, as do the intellectuals. Its bud and bloom is admired by all, offered on altars, adored as sacred, as are the ones who have lifted themselves into the air and sun and are spiritually unfolded, open to the Divine Light. Yes, all men and women in every society have a chance to become perfect, for all mature and are nurtured by the muddy soil beneath the flowing waters. These 1,080 verses explain in detail just how this is to be done.

Many stories are told about the great ones, the rishis, pandits, seers, saints and sages in the religious literature of India who are the stabilizers of the community and the silent voice whispering in the ear of prominent leaders, the secret advisors of kings and their ministers.

In each *yuga*, millennium, century and decade, there are different ratios of the combinations of the instinctive person, the instinctive-intellectual, the superconsciously intellectual, and the superconscious, intuitive seers. In this Kali Yuga, instinctive people predominate. In the Sat Yuga, superconscious people lead by virtue of their wisdom, not necessarily by holding any official office. They see, ponder, deliberate and

A sandalwood model of the graceful 133-foot-tall statue of Saint Tiruvalluvar carved in granite at Kanya Kumari, South India

The massive stone chariot enshrining a statue of Saint Tiruvalluvar in Chennai

guide the intellectuals and are generally listened to. In each yuga, millennium or century, a nation, state, city or localized community can be dominated by one of these three kinds of groups. It is of these three that our saint speaks.

It is good for leadership to be careful that the moods and emotions of people don't drop into the lower, instinctive energies. The weaver explains this fully, for he has understood the nature of being human. *Sanroor* is the weaver's Tamil word for the perfect, or superconscious, far-seeing and intuitive man or woman, the one who lives a disciplined and noble life and keeps the instinctive and intellectual natures in line with dharma. In olden days, rishis guided the monarchs, who in turn guided these various strata of people, according each one their right tasks and place in the community. Yes, the weaver assures us we can have a Sat Yuga today, a golden age in our community, by understanding and then putting into action the wisdom contained between the covers of this remarkable book.

The Tirukural in Modern South India

Happily, this scripture is not just an obsolete relic of India's past, but is a living light of her present. In fact, there is a great resurgence of interest in the weaver's work. At the dawning of a new millennium in the West (remembering that the Hindu calendar under which the weaver worked calls the Christian-era year 2000 by another name, the Tamil year *Pramathin*, 5101), a monument to rival the Statue of Liberty in New York is being raised in South India, a 133-foot-high stone masterpiece of Saint Tiruvalluvar. As this book goes to press, the statue is being installed at Kanya Kumari, the tip of India, where the Indian Ocean, Bay of Bengal and Arabian Sea meet. Designed by Tiru V. Ganapati Sthapati, a traditional temple architect and our own architect for the San Marga Iraivan

Temple in Hawaii, the sculpture is a testimony to the stone carver's art, featuring massive stone doors moving on stone hinges, free-swinging stone chains, stone bells that ring resonantly and delicate stone lattices.

At the Valluvar monument, visitors can walk up stone stairs and out onto the saint's outstretched arm. The best stone-workers of South India, demonstrating the vitality of their ancient craft, were assembled to carve the statue of the weaver-saint that now rises out of the ocean on a small island next to the Vivekananda Rock Memorial, a quarter-mile offshore. The statue of the weaver-saint at Kanya Kumari is expected to swell the numbers of the 1.5 million pilgrims who come each year to Kanya Kumari to visit the Vivekananda Memorial. Valluvar's gaze from Minor Rock Island will be able to survey the entire expanse of Mother India, from the Kanya Kumari temple, right up to the Himalayas, blessing the land. While America's Statue of Liberty is a metal monument to political freedom and social promise, Tiruvalluvar stands as a stone statement of political wisdom, social duty and the spiritual promise of dharma.

In 1976, Tiru Ganapati Sthapati completed another monument to Tiruvalluvar, the Valluvar Kottam in Chennai. The three-acre park features the 1,330 verses inscribed on giant polished granite slabs, and a giant stone and concrete replica of a temple chariot, pulled by magnificent elephants, which enshrines a large statue of Tiruvalluvar. The Kottam is today a popular pilgrimage and family outing destination.

On the grounds of Kauai Aadheenam in Hawaii we have installed two large stone statues, made in Mahabalipuram in Tamil Nadu by the famed Neelameham Sthapati, one of Saint Tiruvalluvar and the other of Rishi Tirumular.

There is nothing in Western schools, with the possible exception of nursery rhymes, that compares with the universal memorization of the *Tirukural* in South India. Reflecting the

Tamilians' special affection for the weaver's couplets, schools in Tamil Nadu, the southernmost state, always include the weaver's poems (of the first two parts, on dharma and wealth, not the third on love) in school texts from grade one to twelve. *Tirukural* memorization contests are conducted in schools, with hundreds of thousands of students vying to memorize the most, with public recitations and big awards ceremonies each year. Here the state government has declared a paid holiday the day after Pongal festival, January 14, in memory of their eminent saint, Tiruvalluvar. Even in the marketplace you find the weaver's wisdom, on posters in store windows, in institutional literature, on the sides of the buses, and there are buses here as nowhere in the world. The media, too, loves the *Tirukural*. It is read each day on radio stations. Fictional stories are written for television based on a few couplets. Magazine and newspaper articles feature the praises of Tiruvalluvar. College courses and multi-media CDs are available on the subject, and literary seminars abound. In recent years, *Tirukural* websites are proliferating, some of which include audio readings of the verses.

Yes! It is only fitting that the *Tirukural* play a dynamic part in today's world, for through all our experience we have discovered no other work from any culture, from anytime in history, from any place on Earth that in even the least way holds a candle to the *Tirukural*. It is one of a kind, a gift from "up-down," a spiritual, intellectual, emotional guide map for all mankind. There are those who would say that the *Tirukural* is out of date and has long spent its time, now that communism, secularism and democracy are in vogue, now that turmoil is an accepted way of life, now that villages have become cities. We sincerely feel that this new edition and the guiding introductions between each section give new life, an onward, "into-the-future" look for all humanity seeking wise direction in a world that has too little of it.

About this Modern English Translation

This edition of the *Tirukural* was two decades in the preparation. While in Sri Lanka in 1975, I directed two of my *sannyasins* to bring into American English the essential meaning of 1,080 of the weaver's verses. There had never been a translation in modern American English, and I saw a need, even among educated Tamils, for a more accessible edition, one that spoke to them and to their children (who do not know their native language) in today's language, not in the language of so long ago. At Kauai Aadheenam, our monastery in Hawaii, they worked in the hours before dawn for many years to provide such a translation. They sat together at Siva's feet, in our Kadavul Nataraja Temple, and slowly brought out the meaning, refining it, then polishing it, then perfecting it.

I gave them five objectives for their work: 1) to be faithful to the original Tamil in meaning and style; 2) to be clear and understandable; 3) to be brief whenever possible so as to capture the saint's succinct style; 4) to be subtle and profound; and, finally; 5) to have the verses as graceful and refined in American English as they are in Tamil. This was not an easy *sadhana*, as you can imagine. It was further complicated by the fact that the text was written twenty centuries ago in a classical form of Tamil that is difficult even for native speakers to understand today. The two *sannyasins* had to meditate on exactly what the saint meant, for often his verses are obscure, recondite and subtle. They had to capture the same meaning, the same insight, to discover the same area of consciousness the saint held as he wrote down those syllables. And then they had to speak out the perception in the vernacular of our day. Realizing that much meaning would be lost if the attempt was made to forge rhyming verses in the translation, I instructed my *sannyasins* not to attempt that, but to work in prose instead. Following these directions produced

E.M. SETHURAMAN

Old-style books: *Olai leaf manuscripts archived at the Mahamaho-padhyaya Dr. U.V. Swaminatha Iyer Library, Besant Nagar, Chennai*

quotable wisdom for lectures, discussions with friends and family, and anywhere where people meet to observe and solve human and social issues. We concluded the final reading and careful editing of *Tirukural* on the 11th of February, 1999.

The art depicting the 108 subjects of this book is all the work of Tiru A. Manivelu of Chennai, a traditionally-trained craftsman who is renowned for having spent his life painting the presiding Deities in all of the sacred temple shrines throughout India. Working with my *sannyasins*, Tiru Mani-velu captured the essence of each chapter in watercolors, a challenge that required many months of diligent effort and interpretation. His style is that of the deep South, and partic-ularly of the Tamil people and culture.

The *Tirukural* is composed of extremely terse heptametic verses, with the seven metrical feet split as four in one line

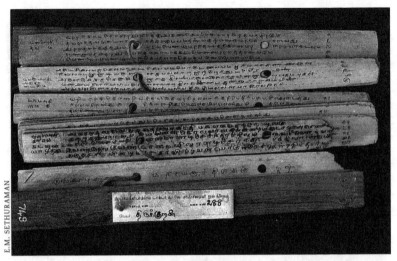

E.M. SETHURAMAN

Tirukural **treasure:** *The Tirukural was preserved through the centuries by being recopied as needed on olai leaf manuscripts such as this one. (Size is 12¾ x 1½"—Swaminatha Iyer Library, Chennai.)*

(usually the first) and three in the other. Here, for example, is what the very first *kural* in the book looks and sounds like.

அகர முதல எழுத்தெல்லாம் ஆதி
பகவன் முதற்றே உலகு.

Akara muthala eluth ellam Athi
Bhagavan muthatre ulaku.

"A" is the first and source of all the letters. Even so is
God Primordial the first and source of all the world.

Of course, the verses were not written on paper, but etched on *olai* leaves with a sharp stylus, then rubbed with lamp black to color the etching. By the structural style of the *Kural* one is reminded of the *Brahma Sutras* or the Greek epigrammatic masterpieces. With subjects of predicates often only implied, the reader is left to intuit the meaning, and the result is a wide range of legitimate interpretation. This is not helped by the age of the language itself, differing from modern Tamil as much or more as Chaucer's Middle English in the *Canterbury Tales* differs from our language today. One way that translators often chose to indicate to readers what the venerable author actually said and what he implied was to place implied words or phrases in parentheses—a device useful to scholars but cumbersome for the average reader and therefore not used in our translation.

With the *Tirukural's* great popularity, there have arisen many translations through the years. When my swamis began this work, there existed roughly twenty-five English versions; and by the time they finished, another four or five had emerged. The work of other translators sheds an interesting light on ours, giving the reader a sense of the several ways, adept and inept, that the weaver's words have been wrought into English. Only the best among translations were selected for comparison here. They are, of course, also the most renowned. Three were chosen to exemplify the prose approach, those being Rev. W.H. Drew (1840); Tiru G. Vanmikanathan (1984), a dear friend we knew well in those early days; and Tiru P.S. Sundaram (1989). Another two were selected to represent what is undoubtedly the most difficult approach, that of rhymed poetry, these being the famous work of Rev. G.U. Pope (1886) and the more recent couplets of Tiru K.M. Balasubramuniam (1962). Our gratitude to all translators who have gone before us. Here, now, are verses 15, 53, 90, 92, 105, 229 and 252, as translated in our American English edition (abbreviated W.W. and in bold type), and in the works of Drew (W.D.), Pope (G.P.), Balasubramuniam (K.B), Vanmikanathan (G.V.) and Sundaram (P.S.).

Verse 15: The Importance of Rain

W.W.   **It is rain that ruins, and it is rain again
that raises up those it has ruined.**

W.D.   Rain by its absence ruins men;
and by its existence restores them to fortune.

G.P.   'Tis rain works all: it ruin spreads, then timely aid supplies;
as, in the happy days before, it bids the ruined rise.

K.B.   It is the rain which causeth ruin and it is the rain
which, as the prop of ruined ones, doth lift them up again.

G.V.   That which ruins the peasants, and, acting as succor
to the ruined peasants, revives them—all that is rain.

P.S.   It is rain which ruins men; it is also rain
which lifts them up.

Verse 53, The Good Wife

W.W.   **What does a man lack if his wife is worthy?
And what does he possess if she is lacking worth?**

W.D.   If his wife be eminent (in virtue) what does (that man) not possess? If she be without excellence, what does (he) possess?

G.P.   There is no lack within the house, where wife in worth excels,
there is no luck within the house, where wife dishonored dwells.

K.B.   What is the good one lacks with one's own wife of virtuous birth?
What is the good one hath with one's own wife devoid of worth?

G.V.   What is lacking, provided the wife excels in those accomplishments? What is there, if the wife does not do so?

P.S.   With a good wife, what is lacking?
And when she is lacking, what is good?

Verse 90, Hospitality

W.W.   **The delicate *anicham* flower withers when merely smelled.
But an unwelcome look is enough to wither the heart of a guest.**

W.D.   As the *anicham* flower fades in smelling,
so fades the guest when the face is turned away.

G.P.   The flower of *anicha* withers 'way if you do but its fragrance inhale; if the face of the host cold welcome convey, the guest's heart within him will fail.

K.B.   Whilst soft *anichcha* flower doth wither away but when 'tis smelt,
       a wry-faced look askance will cause one's guests to wither and melt.

G.V.   The *anichcham* flower will wilt on being smelled;
       the guest will wilt on being merely looked at with a wry face.

P.S.   The *aniccam* withers when smelt;
       a cold look withers a guest.

Verse 92, Speaking Pleasant Words

W.W.   **Better than a gift given with a joyous heart
       are sweet words spoken with a cheerful smile.**

W.D.   Sweet speech with a cheerful countenance
       is better than a gift made with a joyous mind.

G.P.   A pleasant word with beaming smile's preferred,
       even to gifts with liberal heart conferred.

K.B.   Ev'n more than gifting off with gladdened heart it is worthwhile
       to greet the guests with pleasing words along with welcome smile.

G.V.   If one becomes a man of pleasant mien and sweet speech,
       it is superior to giving with all one's heart.

P.S.   More pleasing than a gracious gift
       are sweet words heartfelt.

Verse 105, Gratitude

W.W.   **Help rendered another cannot be measured by the extent of the
       assistance given. Its true measure is the worth of the recipient.**

W.D.   The benefit itself is not the measure of the benefit;
       the worth of those who have received it is its measure.

G.P.   The kindly aid's extent is of its worth no measure true,
       its worth is as the worth of him to whom the act you do.

K.B.   No turn for help received is e'er a measure for each measure.
       It is dependent on the noble recipient's pleasure.

G.V.   A reciprocal help is not to be limited to the extent of the help
       received; its extent is governed by the nobility of the character of
       the recipient of the original help.

P.S.   Not according to the aid but its receiver
       is its recompense determined.

Verse 229, Charity

W.W. **More bitter than even a beggar's bread is the meal
of the miser who hoards his wealth and eats alone.**

W.D. Solitary and unshared eating for the sake of filling up one's
own riches is certainly much more unpleasant than begging.

G.P. They keep their garners full, for self alone the board they spread;
'tis greater pain, be sure, than begging daily bread!

K.B. Then e'en the begging far more painful is the act of one
who eats one's hoarded meal by oneself, sharing that with none.

G.V. More repugnant than begging is eating all alone
in order to make up the shortfall in the target of one's savings.

P.S. To eat alone what one has hoarded
is worse than begging.

Verse 252, Abstaining from Eating Meat

W.W. **Riches cannot be found in the hands of the thriftless, nor
can compassion be found in the hearts of those who eat meat.**

W.D. As those possess no property who do not take care of it,
so those possess no kindness who feed on flesh.

G.P. No use of wealth have they who guard not their estate;
no use of grace have they with flesh who hunger sate.

K.B. The blessings of the wealth are not for those who fail to guard.
The blessings of compassion for the flesh-eaters are barred.

G.V. Profiting by wealth is not for those who do not cherish it;
profiting by charity is not for those who eat flesh.

P.S. The fruits of wealth are not for the wastrel.
Nor of grace for a meat-eater.

We have omitted the third part of the *Tirukural* from this
translation for several reasons. Firstly, as monks, the section
was too sensual to allow our involvement in the translation.
Secondly, the book is designed in large part to engage and interest youth and children, and this section seemed inappro-
priate for them. Thirdly, it frankly seemed less relevant to
modern life and experience, being an ingenuous romantic di-

alog. Finally, these last twenty-five chapters are so much out of character with the rest of the book that we even wondered whether they might be the work of another author. The structure, language and approach is completely different from all that has preceded it. Even the subtlety of thought is not nearly so great. There is also a logic that says that Tiruvalluvar wrote 108 chapters because of the auspiciousness and meaning of the number 108 in Hindu tradition. The names of God are 108. The number of beads on a *mala* for the performance of *japa*, repetition of God's name, are 108. Note that 108 adds up to nine, so auspicious in Hindu numerology, and 1,080, the total of all the verses in the first two sections of the work, does as well, providing a built-in mystical blessing. That he would have composed 108 chapters is a logical assumption, and that the style changes so radically is, to us, a further negative indication.

This last section, called *Kamatupal* in Tamil, deals with passion and love. Chapters 109 to 115 are about a young man and a maiden who fall in love and flee into the forest to live, without benefit of a formal marriage. Chapters 116 to 133 are about their life as man and wife, about the pains of their temporary separations, about the merits of feminine wiles and coyness and the pangs of jealousy. All the verses are the spoken words of one of four characters, the man, his lover and their two intimate friends.

To give readers a sense of the 25 chapters not included in this book, here is a selection of verses from the translation by our friend, Tiru G. Vanmikanathan.

1081   "(He to himself on seeing her for the first time) Is she a nymph? Or a rare kind of peacock? Or woman with heavy earrings? Sorely perplexed is my soul."

1167   "(She to her lady-in-waiting who said that one should swim across the sea of passion with self-restraint as a float) I have swum about in the cruel sea of passion and cannot find the shore. Even at midnight, I am all by myself."

1261   "(She, out of eager desire to meet him again) My eyes have lost
their luster and have become weak watching for his coming; my
fingers are worn out going over the markings on the wall keeping
tally on the days that have passed since his departure."

1114-5 "(He to her lady-in-waiting after leaving the bedroom) I told her 'I
love you more than anyone else.' She immediately went into the
sulks, crying, 'More than whom? More than whom?' I told her, 'I
will never leave you in this life.' At once her eyes filled with tears
for fear that I may desert her in other lives."

1171   "(She to her lady-in-waiting, who said: 'Your eyes have lost their
beauty through weeping ; you should control yourself.') Is it not
through these eyes showing my lover to me that I suffer this unremitting illness? Why do they weep now?"

1172   "These collyrium-painted eyes which looked on (my lover that
day) without inquiring (into the consequences), why do they now
suffer torture without realising (their fault)?"

1173   "These were the eyes that rushed to see (my lover that day); today
they themselves weep. This is laughable."

1174   "After bringing upon me this unbearable interminable malady,
these collyrium-painted eyes have so dried up that they can no
longer weep."

1175   "My eyes which caused this love-sickness which the sea cannot
match, now suffer torment without closing in sleep."

1176   "Oh, it is delightful indeed that these eyes which caused these dis-
eases in me have themselves come to this state."

1177   "Let these eyes which longingly and meltingly looked unceasingly
at my lover (that day) suffer and suffer (today) and become bereft
of tears in them."

1179   "(She to L.i.W., who said: 'You should compose yourself, and your
eyes should close in sleep.') If he does not come, they will not sleep;
and, even if he comes, they will not sleep (for fear of his going
away): in either case, the eyes undergo unendurable suffering."

1211   "(She to L.i.W. on dreaming of a messenger to her husband) How
shall I entertain the dream which has come bearing a message
from my husband?"

Oddly, it is traditional in Hindu architecture to have licentious images in view as one approaches a temple. It was explained to me, as a wondering young man, that to stimulate the sexual nature through thought in turn heightened the quality of worship. This means that once stimulated a little upon entering the temple, that same energy would pass up the spine during worship and quiet the mind. All this was explained to me by Tiru Kandiah Chettiar, who adopted me into his family during my 1949 stay in Sri Lanka. He told me that this was also done in certain books, like the *Tirukural*. It was, he explained, a literary tradition to add a sensual last chapter to a book, perhaps centuries after the book was written, to capture readers. He said that some scholars and elders postulate that the section on love was added to the *Tirukural*, with many sensual verses, to bring readers into the weaver's more serious subjects.

How to Apply the Verses to Life

As you go through the verses in this holy book, take in the essence of what is being said. Try to refrain from analyzing each word or phrase. Endeavor to catch the spirit of a land, a government, a religion, a people free from toil, free from conflict and free to express themselves, to thrive and grow. Thousands upon thousands have approached these verses as a friendly guide to life's challenges, in the following way. While holding the book between both hands, keeping an open mind, think "Aum, Aum, Aum," and on the third recitation of *Aum* open the book at random. The first verse your eyes fall upon becomes your meditation and insight for the day, answering the questions weighing upon your mind. If this is done for 365 days for several years, the essence of this amazing seer's wise observation becomes imbedded deep in the subconscious, thus becoming an intrinsic part of your life.

On days that we are feeling empty, with no hope for the future, the answers of upliftment will be found herein. On days when life is full of abundance and free from sorrow, close direction on how to contain and maintain this treasured estate may be found. To those who are statesmen, corporate heads, professionals in finance and medicine, engineering and the military, presidents, ministers, governors, mayors and executives of every kind, answers are abundant as to how to maintain and advance their vision of service, their personal life and career; for the weaver understood well, even then, how to progress from success to success, and how to fall from favor, how to gain and lose wealth, how to nurture and offend friends. Enjoy *Weaver's Wisdom* as your map for a most rewarding future.

In fact, one of the striking revelations readers may have as they go through this text is how little has changed in two millennia. People basically have the same worries, face the same fears and personal challenges, struggle with the same weaknesses and foibles, cherish the same aspirations for goodness and nobility. And, sadly, they have the same propensity for dishonesty and corruption. How much we are today like the people the weaver writes about is a most stunning fact. Consequently, we may be startled at the aptness of this old Indian craftsman's words, for they apply fully to us today as mankind enters the third millennium since the work's creation. There is, indeed, not a single *kural* that seems outmoded or irrelevant to our modern life. That in itself is an amazing fact!

We would strongly suggest that you teach these gems to the children. The weaver's advice and admonition, coming from the world's most ancient faith and culture, will enrich every child's understanding of goodness, right conduct and right thought. It is one of the most sagacious scriptures in the world today. It should be memorized, especially by small children, at least one verse carefully chosen by mother and father, from each of the 108 chapters, as a beginning. This will create a positive conscience for their inner decisions, guiding how they will conduct themselves through life. Small children all through Sri Lanka and South India memorize the *Holy Kural* so as to chant it verse after verse. Many can recite all 1,330 verses by heart. This gives them a code of living that remains with them the rest of their lives.

We all know that it is crucial that children be given the benefit of strong principles from a very early age. This is especially true in these times when television stories, plots and scenes present the prevalent dissipated code of living. It is essential that the *Tirukural's* do's and don'ts be carried over for the next generation with pride and persistence so that our descendants, the heirs of the future, are benefited by these age-old insights into the universal laws of dharma.

Read to your children one chapter of the book aloud each day, or have the older ones read. This is best done in the morning after *puja*, at meal time or just before sleep, to let its wisdom penetrate deeply and enliven their inner knowing, giving the needed tools to make their own decisions in the right way. This responsibility rests with all parents and all who teach children, and who should, therefore, feel free to draw upon this storehouse of ethical living.

Another way to bring this book to life in your everyday life is to commit its verses to memory and meditate upon them. And in your daily conversations, quote freely from them as your very own. You will sound wise if you remember and share these jewels, not mentioning where you learned them. One of the greatest benefits of this scripture is to guide our actions and our thoughts, to direct our purpose in life and refine our interactions with our fellow man. Problems can be resolved in the light of the saint's wisdom. If something is going wrong in your life—stress, conflict, disharmony—bring the forces back into harmony by studying the *Tirukural* and applying its knowledge. That is perhaps its main function—to perfect and protect our lives by preventing mistakes that can cause unhappy *karma*, by preventing erroneous attitudes that bring unnecessary sorrow into our experience. Yet, there is nothing in the *Tirukural* that *has* to be obeyed. Each couplet contains such insight, however, that we are drawn to it and want to obey. But, having said all that, memorize at least one verse from each chapter. Then on special occasions or during *Tirukural* contests you will come forth shining.

Use *Weaver's Wisdom* as a book of guidance or divination, not unlike other great works, such as the Chinese *I-Ching*, drawing on your innate intuitive powers, which everyone has. Hold the book between both hands in a prayerful posture. Mentally ask for the answer, the solution, the inspiration needed. Chant *Aum* (or your own favorite prayer) three times and then open the book. And there, the first verse your eyes fall upon, is your Indian fortune cookie of the day, any day, many all through the day, day after day. They will, we must warn, make you fat with wisdom. The first *kural* the eyes fall upon has proven time and again to tens of thousands to contain the needed solution, direction, insight and advice.

Let's face it, everyone has reached for that fortune cookie after a delicious Chinese meal, wondering before it was opened if it could really, possibly, magically apply to his life at that moment. I know I have. Then, thinking about the few short lines on that little, hard-to-read paper, we wonder just how, or how much, it really connects to our inner question, or if, indeed, it was a part of our karma to pick up that particular cookie. Or were they all the same? Then, if the message seems to not apply, we think it must be random. So, we say, "Let's all share out loud our fortune cookie's message." We do and did so many times, and more often than not, find the messages pertinent to each of us at the table at that moment.

I encourage all readers to use this scripture to provide

guidelines for effective and virtuous action in your life and that of your family. It can be your refuge in times of confusion, a source of inspiration when you feel less than inspired, a central hub around which the endless play of Lord Siva's *maya* revolves. It can be studied to comprehend the nature of virtue and the difficulties caused by transgressing virtue's natural laws.

In conclusion to the beginning of the book that we have labored on with great love and tenacity, it is important to note that we have modeled our entire international organization on the weaver's advice, admonitions, the never-ending directives, which has helped us make decisions in uncompromising situations to uncompromise them into solutions. We highly recommend the wisdom of the weaver to be a vital part of your life now as it has been ours.

Love and blessings to you from this and inner worlds,

Satguru Sivaya Subramuniyaswami
162nd Jagadacharya of the Nandinatha
Sampradaya's Kailasa Parampara,
Guru Mahasannidhanam,
Kauai Aadheenam, Kauai, Hawaii
Satguru Purnima, July, 27, 1999, Tamil Year 5101, Pramathin

Arattuppal

அறத்துப்பால்

Part I

On Virtue

Paayiram
பாயிரம்

பிறவிப் பெருங்கடல் நீந்துவர் நீந்தார்
இறைவன் அடிசேரா தார்.

Section I
Prologue

KURAL 10
The boundless ocean of births can be crossed, indeed,
but not without intimate union with Infinity's Holy Feet.

HERE NOW ARE THE PUNGENT OPENING VERSES, FILLED WITH FOUNDATIONAL KNOWLEDGE FOR THE BEGINNING NOVICE AND THE ADVANCED PANDIT. God supreme is explained in no uncertain terms, beginning with the primordial AUM, the Primal Sound of the universe, the A of many alphabets. Nothing would exist without the constant resonant resounding AUM, the Soundless Sound, the impulse of creation, ever emanating from the Cosmic Dance of God Siva, the source of all three worlds. Throughout the first ten *kurals*, one is encouraged to worship, to worship, to worship and thus soften negative karmas. Speaking of the Holy Feet, the weaver tells us of the ancient tradition so imbedded in Indian culture that even today touching the feet of a holy icon, a swami, sadhu, elder and one's mother and father is a gesture of deepest respect.

It is in these first four chapters that the weaver creates the warp, the strong, taut strands that stretch from one end of the loom to the other—as in the *Vedas* the priests' mantras are described as the warp connecting this world with the heavenly Sivaloka—each strand's color indicating a pattern of excellence yet to come. This first section of *Weaver's Wisdom* tells us of the importance of God Siva's Holy Feet, of rain, of renunciates and of virtuous living, called dharma. Here and in many chapters to come, reincarnation, *punarjanma*, is set forth in a most pragmatic way. In the tenth *kural*, the weaver tells of the boundless ocean of births that can be crossed only when one has become bound to Siva's Feet.

In chapter two, the author shows that in his day man was a vital, responsible part of ecology, inseparably entangled within it. This reverence for the environment forms another group of threads in the warp of our weaver's pattern yet to be unfolded. The Abrahamic religions, upon which historically most scientists based their postulations, brought to mankind the attitude that man is not a part of ecology, but set apart from it, created to control and selfishly exploit it. This perspective has led to mountainous problems: pollution, waste and deforestation, extermination of whole species, drought and much, much more. The weaver speaks eloquently of rain in chapter two. And in verses throughout the book he says that good behavior of the people brings rain, hence wealth, and *adharmic,* or unvirtuous, behavior brings drought, hence poverty, leading to famine. A point is made that should rain fail, the worship within the temples and home shrines of God and the Gods would cease, and the joyous festivals, which during that time were many, would be held no more.

Chapter three creates another warp on the weaver's loom— the taut threads of the renunciate and ascetic—for in his day it was the sadhus, swamis and rishis who guided community leaders and individual seekers on the right path, and kept the monarch on the side of dharma, divine law and order. In verse 21 the weaver tells how the *Vedas* exalt the greatness of virtuous renunciates, and in verse 29 he explains that pious men who have compassion for all life are looked up to and respected as the priestly ones.

Chapter four, "Asserting Virtue's Power," defines the fourth set of strands in the pale-colored, many-threaded warp on the weaver's word loom. This completes the four-part set of lengthwise strands and forms the base of the cloth: the white threads of Sivaness; the translucent blues of rain, or *akasha;* the saffron-yellow threads of sacrifice and renunciation; and the violet rays of virtue. These are the four kinds of grace we must have in life: God, rain, holy ones and virtue.

Chapter five begins the threads that crisscross the warp to form the weft. These are the rich-colored threads of virtue and wealth that the weaver uses to create the tapestry of life.

அகர முதல எழுத்தெல்லாம் ஆதி
பகவன் முதற்றே உலகு.

Praising God

KURAL 1

"A" is the first and source of all the letters. Even so is
God Primordial the first and source of all the world.

KURAL 2

What has learning profited a man, if it has not led him
to worship the Good Feet of Him who is pure knowledge itself?

KURAL 3

The Supreme dwells within the lotus of the heart. Those who reach
His Splendid Feet dwell enduringly within unearthly realms.

KURAL 4

Draw near the Feet of Him who is free of desire
and aversion, and live forever free of suffering.

KURAL 5

Good and bad, delusion's dual deeds, do not cling to those
who delight in praising the Immutable, Worshipful One.

KURAL 6

A long and joyous life rewards those who remain firmly
on the faultless path of Him who controls the five senses.

KURAL 7

They alone dispel the mind's distress
who take refuge at the Feet of the Incomparable One.

KURAL 8

They alone can cross life's other oceans who take refuge
at the Feet of the Gracious One, Himself an Ocean of Virtue.

KURAL 9

The head which cannot bow before the Feet of the Possessor of
eight infinite powers is like the senses lacking the power to perceive.

KURAL 10

The boundless ocean of births can be crossed, indeed,
but not without intimate union with Infinity's Holy Feet.

கெடுப்பதூஉங் கெட்டார்க்குச் சார்வாய்மற் றாங்கே
எடுப்பதூஉம் எல்லாம் மழை.

The Importance of Rain

KURAL 11
It is the unfailing fall of rain that sustains the world.
Therefore, look upon rain as the nectar of life.

KURAL 12
Rain produces man's wholesome food;
and rain itself forms part of his food besides.

KURAL 13
Though oceanic waters surround it, the world will be deluged
by hunger's hardships if the billowing clouds betray us.

KURAL 14
When clouds withhold their watery wealth,
farmers cease to ply their plows.

KURAL 15
It is rain that ruins, and it is rain again
that raises up those it has ruined.

KURAL 16
Unless raindrops fall from the sky,
not a blade of green grass will rise from the earth.

KURAL 17
The very nature of oceans, though vast, would diminish
if clouds ceased to take up water and replenish rain's gifts.

KURAL 18
Should the heavens dry up, worship here of the heavenly ones
in festivals and daily rites would wither.

KURAL 19
Unless the heavens grant their gifts, neither the giver's generosity
nor the ascetic's detachment will grace this wide world.

KURAL 20
No life on Earth can exist without water,
and water's ceaseless flow cannot exist without rain.

ஒழுக்கத்து நீத்தார் பெருமை விழுப்பத்து
வேண்டும் பனுவல் துணிவு.

The Greatness of Renunciates

KURAL 21
The Scriptures exalt above every other good
the greatness of virtuous renunciates.

KURAL 22
Attempting to speak of the renunciate's magnitude is like
numbering all the human multitudes who have ever died.

KURAL 23
Behold those who have weighed the dual nature of things and
followed the renunciate's way. Their greatness illumines the world.

KURAL 24
He whose firm will, wisdom's goading hook, controls his five senses
is a seed that will flourish in the fields of Heaven.

KURAL 25
Such is the power of those who subdue the five senses, that even Indra,
sovereign of spacious Heaven's celestials, suffered their curse.

KURAL 26
The magnificent ones are they who can dispatch the most
difficult tasks; the insignificant ones are they who cannot.

KURAL 27
Touch, taste, sight, smell and hearing are the senses—
he who controls these five magically controls the world.

KURAL 28
Their own subtle sayings reveal to the world
the greatness of men whose words prove prophetic.

KURAL 29
It is impossible to endure, even for a second, the wrath of those
who have scaled and stand upon the mountain called virtue.

KURAL 30
Pious men are called the priestly ones,
for they are clothed in robes of compassion for all life.

ஒல்லும் வகையான் அறவினை ஓவாதே
செல்லும் வாயெல்லாஞ் செயல்.

Asserting Virtue's Power

KURAL 31

Virtue yields Heaven's honor and Earth's wealth.
What is there then that is more fruitful for a man?

KURAL 32 •

There is nothing more rewarding than virtue,
nor anything more ruinous than its neglect.

KURAL 33

Be unremitting in the doing of good deeds;
do them with all your might and by every possible means.

KURAL 34

Keep the mind free of impurity. That alone is
the practice of virtue. All else is nothing but empty display.

KURAL 35

Virtue is living in such a way that one does not fall
into these four: envy, anger, greed and unsavory speech.

KURAL 36

Don't tell yourself you'll be wise enough to practice virtue tomorrow.
Do it now, for it will be your deathless companion when you die.

KURAL 37

It is utterly superfluous to inquire about virtue's benefits, so
evident in the difference between the palanquin's rider and bearer.

KURAL 38

Not allowing a day to pass without doing some good
is a boulder that will block your passage on the path to rebirth.

KURAL 39

Only virtuous deeds abound in true joy.
All other deeds are empty and devoid of distinction.

KURAL 40

Virtue is merely that which should be done in life,
and vice is merely that which should be avoided.

Illaraviyal
இல்லறவியல்

Section II

The Way of
The Householder

KURAL 44

The posterity of householders who gather wealth without
misdeeds and share meals without miserliness will never perish.

IN INDIA IN THE DAYS BEFORE THE CHRISTIAN ERA, THERE WERE NO PAGANS. IN THE DAYS BEFORE THE ISLAMIC ERA, THERE WERE NO INFIDELS. IN THE DAYS BEfore contemporary science, religion was respected, the air was not polluted, nor was the water; the lands flourished, and family life was strong. Extended families worked together, obedient to the laws of the land, to the religion that guided them through life; and to their parents, grandparents and great grandparents homage was given. "Those who bear children of blameless character will be untouched by evil for seven births," the weaver declares, alluding to reincarnation and encouraging prayer before conception to reach up to the upper worlds rather than down to the nether worlds to embody a soul. In Indian cultures dedicated to ahimsa, corporal punishment in homes and schools was not as much in vogue as nowadays, and in the purest of traditional ashrams it was totally unacceptable as a systematic method of education.

Home life was strong. Parents loved their children and spoke with them of God, Gods, gurus and of the laws governing family life that this section of our weaver's weft explains. It is here that praise is given for well-behaved youth who make parents ponder, "By what great austerities did we merit such a child?" The weaver puts great stress on hospitality, explaining that the whole purpose of maintaining a home and earning wealth is to provide hospitality to guests. Speaking words of praise with a cheerful smile, gratitude, giving help in the hour of need, possessing self-control, virtuous conduct and gracious hospitality—all this was the way of the day.

He offers a new look at wealth, observing that if one is profoundly impoverished yet remains just, the world will not regard him as poor. A good lesson for us in today's world. In the chapter on self-control he alludes to the Brahmaloka, or highest heaven, explaining that self-control will place one among the Gods. Then he refers to the Narakaloka, or lowest Hell, by saying the lack of self-control leads to deepest darkness.

The weaver says, "Morality is the birthright of high families, while immoral conduct's legacy is lowly birth," inferring that what was done in a past life determines the joys or pains in the next, and what is done in this life will affect the one to follow. Adultery was a "no no" then as it is today: "Hatred, sin, fear and disgrace—these four never forsake the man who commits adultery." This wisdom seems to be drowned in the free-flowing freedom of expressive life that today floods the world, but now we may turn to *Weaver's Wisdom*, pulled from the deep past and dressed in American English and modern Tamil to persist into the future of futures.

He explains what great goodness the Goddess of Wealth, Lakshmi, will do when envious, inharmonious conditions arise in the family, saying "Fortune's Goddess, intolerant of those who cannot tolerate other's success, introduces them to her sister, Misfortune, and goes away." On and on, leaving no stone unturned, the weaver explains that we have the duty to form and maintain a society of excellence, and gives us the tools to do so. Any nation or community can benefit from this wisdom, now released into the world language of today.

We have been careful to maintain the weaver's gender distinctions within each verse, as well as the literal meaning of his words. Some might seem surprisingly blunt now and even "sexist," but this was the way of the day then, when men were Gods and women were Goddesses, when gracious ladies were found at home and not raised as men, when men were understanding, kindly, patient and forbearing. We hope those days will be rekindled, and the warmth of the home and the family within it, the true stability of a nation, will return and human communities will enter a bold new beginning.

துறந்தார்க்கும் துவ்வா தவர்க்கும் இறந்தார்க்கும்
இல்வாழ்வான் என்பான் துணை.

Family Life

KURAL 41
He alone may be called a householder who supports
students, elders and renunciates pursuing well their good paths.

KURAL 42
The virtuous householder supports the needs
of renunciates, ancestors and the poor.

KURAL 43
The foremost duty of family life is to serve duly these five:
God, guests, kindred, ancestors and oneself.

KURAL 44
The posterity of householders who gather wealth without misdeeds
and share meals without miserliness will never perish.

KURAL 45
When family life possesses love and virtue,
it has found both its essence and fruition.

KURAL 46
If a man masters the duties of married life,
what further merits could monkhood offer him?

KURAL 47
Among those who strive for liberation, the foremost are they
who live the blessed state of family life as it should be lived.

KURAL 48
The householder dedicated to duty and to aiding
ascetics on their path of penance endures more than they do.

KURAL 49
Domestic life is rightly called virtue. The monastic path,
rightly lived beyond blame, is likewise good.

KURAL 50
He who rightly pursues the householder's life here on Earth
will be rightfully placed among the Gods there in Heaven.

தெய்வம் தொழாஅள் கொழுநன்
தொழுதெழுவாள்
பெய்யெனப் பெய்யும் மழை.

The Good Wife

KURAL 51
She is the helpful wife who possesses the fullness of
domestic virtues and spends within her husband's means.

§KURAL 52
Family life, however full, remains empty
if the wife lacks the lofty culture of the home.

KURAL 53
What does a man lack if his wife is worthy?
And what does he possess if she is lacking worth?

KURAL 54
What is more majestic than a woman
who preserves the prodigious strength of chastity?

KURAL 55
Even the rains will fall at her command
who upon rising worships not God, but her husband.

KURAL 56
A married woman is one who vigilantly guards herself,
cares for her husband and protects their unblemished reputation.

KURAL 57
Why do guardians protect women by confinement
when her own resolute chastity is a woman's best protection?

KURAL 58
A woman deeply devoted to the man who wed her
will be worthy of great rewards in the world where Gods delight.

KURAL 59
Unless the wife pursues praiseworthy purity,
the husband cannot stride before critics like a proud lion.

KURAL 60
It is said a worthy wife is the blessing of a home,
and good children are its precious ornaments.

குழல்இனிது யாழ்இனிது என்பதம் மக்கள்
மழலைச்சொல் கேளா தவர்.

The Blessing of Children

KURAL 61

Of all blessings we know of none greater than
the begetting of children endowed with intelligence.

KURAL 62

Those who bear children of blameless character
will be untouched by evil for seven births.

KURAL 63

It is said that children are a man's real wealth,
and that this wealth is determined by his deeds.

KURAL 64

Far sweeter than divine nectar is simple boiled rice
stirred by the small hands of one's own child.

KURAL 65

The touch of one's children is a delight to the body,
and listening to them chatter is a joy to the ear.

KURAL 66

"Sweet are the sounds of the flute and the lute," say those
who have not heard the prattle of their own children.

KURAL 67

A father benefits his son best by preparing him
to sit at the forefront of learned councils.

KURAL 68

What pleasure it is to human beings everywhere
when their children possess knowledge surpassing their own!

KURAL 69

When a mother hears her son heralded as a good and learned man,
her joy exceeds that of his joyous birth.

KURAL 70

The son's duty to his father is to make the world ask,
"By what great austerities did he merit such a son?"

அன்பு ஈனும் ஆர்வம் உடைமை அதுஈனும்
நண்பென்னும் நாடாச் சிறப்பு.

Possessing Love

KURAL 71

Can any lock keep love confined within,
when the loving heart's tiny tears escape and confess it?

KURAL 72

The unloving belong only to themselves,
but the loving belong to others to their very bones.

KURAL 73

They say it is to know union with love
that the soul takes union with the body.

KURAL 74

Love makes one affectionate toward all,
and affection affords the priceless treasure of friendship.

KURAL 75

They say love's greatness is this: it yields to good families
worldly happiness here and heavenly bliss hereafter.

KURAL 76

The uninformed say love abides with virtuous souls,
unaware that love is also friend to those immersed in vice.

KURAL 77

As the blazing sun dries up a boneless worm,
so does virtue scorch a loveless being.

KURAL 78

Life without love in the heart
is like a sapless tree in a barren desert.

KURAL 79

What good is a body perfect in outer ways,
if inwardly it is impaired by lack of love?

KURAL 80

With love enshrined in the heart, one truly lives.
Without it, the body is but bones encased in skin.

அகனமர்ந்து செய்யாள்
உறையும் முகனமர்ந்து
நல்விருந்து ஓம்புவான் இல்.

Hospitality

KURAL 81
The whole purpose of earning wealth and maintaining
a home is to provide hospitality to guests.

KURAL 82
When a guest is in the home, it is improper to hoard one's meal,
even if it happens to be the nectar of immortality.

KURAL 83
If a man cares daily for those who come to him,
his life will never suffer the grievous ruin of poverty.

KURAL 84
Wealth's Goddess dwells in the hospitable home
of those who host guests with a smiling face.

KURAL 85
If a man eats only after attending to guests' needs,
what further sowing will his fertile fields require?

KURAL 86
The host who, caring for guests, watches hopefully for more,
will himself be a welcomed guest of those whose home is Heaven.

KURAL 87
Charity's merit cannot be measured by gifts given.
It is measured by measuring the receiver's merits.

KURAL 88
Those who never sacrifice to care for guests will later lament:
"We hoarded wealth, estranged ourselves, now none will care for us."

KURAL 89
The poverty of poverties is having plenty yet shunning guests.
Such senselessness is only found in senseless fools.

KURAL 90
The delicate *anicham* flower withers when merely smelled,
but an unwelcome look is enough to wither a guest's heart.

இனிய உளவாக இன்னாத கூறல்
கனியிருப்பக் காய்கவர்ந் தற்று.

Speaking Pleasant Words

KURAL 91

Pleasant words, full of tenderness and devoid of deceit,
fall from the lips of virtuous men.

KURAL 92

Better than a gift given with a joyous heart
are sweet words spoken with a cheerful smile.

KURAL 93

A kindly countenance and sweet words
spoken from the heart are virtue's way.

KURAL 94

Poverty-provoking sorrow will not pursue
those who speak joy-producing words to all they meet.

KURAL 95

Humility and pleasant words are the jewels
that adorn a man; there are none other.

KURAL 96

If a man seeks to do good while speaking sweet words,
his virtues will wax and his vices will wane.

KURAL 97

Words yield spiritual rewards and moral excellence
when they do not wander far from usefulness and agreeableness.

KURAL 98

Sweet speech that is a stranger to pettiness
imparts pleasure not only in this life, but in the next.

§KURAL 99

Why would anyone speak cruel words,
having observed the happiness that kind words confer?

KURAL 100

To utter harsh words when sweet ones would serve
is like eating unripe fruits when ripe ones are at hand.

செய்யாமல் செய்த உதவிக்கு வையகமும்
வானகமும் ஆற்றல் அரிது.

Gratitude

KURAL 101
The bounty of Heaven and Earth are scant repayment
for help rendered though no help was received.

KURAL 102
A kindness done in the hour of need may itself be small,
but in worth it exceeds the whole world.

KURAL 103
When help is given by weighing the recipient's need
and not the donor's reward, its goodness is greater than the sea.

KURAL 104
While aid may outwardly seem as puny as a mustard seed,
those who know will deem it as imposing as a towering palm.

§KURAL 105
Help rendered another cannot be measured by the extent of
assistance given. Its real measure is the recipient's worthiness.

KURAL 106
Never forget fellowship with pure souls,
nor forsake friendship with those who aided you in adversity.

KURAL 107
For seven lives in seven bodies the grateful will remember
friends who relieved their anguish and affliction.

KURAL 108
It is improper to ever forget a kindness,
but good to forget at once an injury received.

KURAL 109
The deadliest injury is effaced the moment
the mind recalls a single kindness received from the injurer.

KURAL 110
Having killed every kind of goodness, one may yet be saved,
but there is no redemption for those who let gratitude die.

சமன்செய்து சீர்தூக்குங் கோல்போல்
அமைந்தொருபால்
கோடாமை சான்றோர்க் கணி.

Impartiality

KURAL 111
Justice may be called good when it acts impartially
toward enemies, strangers and friends.

KURAL 112
The wealth of those who possess justice will not perish;
rather it will be their posterity's soothing security.

KURAL 113
However prosperous it may seem, all wealth gained
by loss of rightness must be relinquished that very day.

KURAL 114
In their offspring one may doubtlessly discern
who are the just and who are the unjust.

KURAL 115
Adversity and prosperity never cease to exist. The adornment
of great men's minds is to remain unswervingly just under both.

KURAL 116
When his heart forsakes fairness and his deeds turn depraved,
a man realizes deep within himself, "I am ruined."

KURAL 117
Though a man is profoundly impoverished,
if he remains just, the world will not regard him as poor.

KURAL 118
To incline to neither side, like a balance scale's level beam,
and thus weigh impartially is the wise one's ornament.

KURAL 119
Speech uttered without bias is integrity,
if no unspoken bias lurks in the heart.

KURAL 120
Those businessmen will prosper whose business
protects as their own the interests of others.

ஒருமையுள் ஆமைபோல் ஐந்தடக்கல் ஆற்றின்
எழுமையும் ஏமாப் புடைத்து.

Possession of Self-Control

KURAL 121
Self-control will place one among the Gods,
while lack of it will lead to deepest darkness.

KURAL 122
Guard your self-control as a precious treasure,
for there is no greater wealth in life than this.

KURAL 123
Comprehending and acquiring self-control
confers upon one the esteem of wise men.

KURAL 124
More imposing than a mountain is the greatness of a man who,
steadfast in domestic life, has mastered self-control.

KURAL 125
Humility is a precious quality in all people,
but it has a rare richness in the rich.

KURAL 126
Like a tortoise withdrawing five limbs into its shell, those who
restrain the five senses in one life will find safe shelter for seven.

KURAL 127
Whatever you may fail to guard, guard well your tongue,
for flawed speech unfailingly invokes anguish and affliction.

KURAL 128
The goodness of all one's virtues can be lost
by speaking even a single word of injury.

KURAL 129
The wound caused by fire heals in its time;
the burn inflicted by an inflamed tongue never heals.

KURAL 130
Virtue will wait in the streets to meet a man
possessed of learning and self-discipline, his anger subdued.

Virtue's Path
அறநெறி

Vice's Way
தீயநெறி

நன்றிக்கு விததாகும் நல்லொழுக்கம்
தீயொழுக்கம்
என்றும் இடும்பை தரும்.

Possession of Virtuous Conduct

KURAL 131
Virtuous conduct leads a man to eminent greatness.
Therefore, it should be guarded as more precious than life itself.

KURAL 132
In your striving, be mindful to preserve good conduct.
In your deliberations, discover it is your staunchest ally.

KURAL 133
Morality is the birthright of high families,
while immoral conduct's legacy is lowly birth.

KURAL 134
If a priest forgets the *Vedas*, he can relearn them.
But if he falls from virtue, his high birth is forever lost.

KURAL 135
Prosperity is not for the envious,
nor is greatness for men of impure conduct.

KURAL 136
The firm-minded never slacken in upholding virtuous conduct,
for they know the miseries brought on by such neglect.

KURAL 137
By honest conduct one achieves honorable eminence,
while corrupt conduct brings one nothing but blame.

KURAL 138
Good conduct is the seed in virtue's field;
wicked conduct's harvest is never-ending sorrow.

KURAL 139
Men who conduct themselves virtuously
are incapable of voicing harmful words, even forgetfully.

KURAL 140
Those who cannot live in harmony with the world,
though they have learned many things, are still ignorant.

பிறன்மனை நோக்காத பேராண்மை சான்றோர்க்கு
அறனொன்றோ ஆன்ற ஒழுக்கு.

Not Coveting Another's Wife

KURAL 141
Those who know virtue's laws and marital rights
never indulge in the folly of desiring another man's wife.

KURAL 142
Among those who stand outside virtue, there is no greater fool
than he who stands with a lustful heart outside another's gate.

KURAL 143
No different from the dead are those who
wickedly desire the wife of a friend.

KURAL 144
Though a man's measure be mountainous, what good is it
if, without the minutest concern, he takes another's wife?

KURAL 145
A man who seduces another man's wife, knowing she is easy,
suffers a shame that neither dies nor diminishes.

KURAL 146
Hatred, sin, fear and disgrace—these four
never forsake the man who commits adultery.

KURAL 147
He is decreed a worthy householder who holds
no desire for the womanly charms of another's wife.

KURAL 148
The chivalry that does not look upon another's wife
is not mere virtue—it is saintly conduct.

KURAL 149
In a world encircled by the awesome sea, to whom do good things
belong? To men never impassioned to caress a married woman.

KURAL 150
Though a man deserts virtue and indulges in vice, he keeps
some decency by not wanting another's wife's womanliness.

அகழ்வாரைத் தாங்கும் நிலம்போலத் தம்மை
இகழ்வாரைப் பொறுத்தல் தலை.

Possession of Forbearance

KURAL 151
Just as the Earth bears those who dig into her,
it is best to bear with those who despise us.

KURAL 152
It is always good to endure injuries done to you,
but to forget them is even better.

KURAL 153
It is impoverished poverty to be inhospitable to guests.
It is stalwart strength to be patient with fools.

KURAL 154
Desiring that greatness should never cease,
let one's conduct foster forbearance.

KURAL 155
Worthless are those who injure others vengefully,
while those who stoically endure are like stored gold.

KURAL 156
The joy of the vengeful lasts only for a day,
but the glory of the forbearing lasts until the end of time.

KURAL 157
Though unjustly aggrieved, it is best to suffer the suffering
and refrain from unrighteous retaliation.

KURAL 158
Let a man conquer by forbearance
those who in their arrogance have wronged him.

KURAL 159
Those who patiently endure rude remarks
possess the rare purity of an ascetic.

KURAL 160
Great are those who suffer fasting's hardships; yet they
are surpassed by those who suffer hard words.

அவ்வித்து அழுக்காறு உடையாளைச் செய்யவள்
தவ்வையைக் காட்டி விடும்.

Avoidance of Envy

KURAL 161
The unenvious heart is to be valued
no less than virtuous conduct itself.

KURAL 162
Among the many precious things a man may acquire,
none surpasses a nature free from envy toward all.

KURAL 163
They say he who is jealous instead of joyous of another's wealth
clearly desires no wealth or virtue of his own.

KURAL 164
Envy will never cause one to commit wrongful deeds
who rightly fathoms the disgrace that follows.

KURAL 165
A man's own envy is foe enough to forge his ruin,
even if he has no other enemies.

KURAL 166
Whoever begrudges another's bounty will watch
his kindred die in poverty, naked and starving.

KURAL 167
Goddess Fortune, intolerant of those who cannot tolerate others'
success, introduces them to her sister, Misfortune, and goes away.

KURAL 168
The wicked one called Envy consumes this world's wealth,
then consigns sinners to those worlds of hellish fire.

KURAL 169
It is worth pondering why good men may be poor
while the envious in heart can prosper.

KURAL 170
There are no envious men who have risen to prosperity.
There are no men free from envy who have fallen from it.

இலமென்று வெ∴குதல் செய்யார் புலம்வென்ற
புன்மையில் காட்சி யவர்.

Avoidance of Covetousness

KURAL 171

In the very attempt to wrongly gain another's wealth,
a man forfeits his family's future and his own faultlessness.

KURAL 172

Those who deem injustice shameful never commit
guilt-yielding deeds driven by money-yielding desires.

KURAL 173

Those who seek immortal bliss will not succumb
to immoral deeds that follow desire for fleeting delights.

KURAL 174

With senses conquered and sight unclouded by depravity,
one will not wish for others' wealth, even in destitution.

KURAL 175

What avails a man's subtle and comprehensive learning,
if, crazed by covetousness, he treats others insensibly?

KURAL 176

Desiring grace and doing his duty, a man who desires wealth
but acquires it wrongly is destroyed nevertheless.

KURAL 177

Do not seek the fortune that greed gathers,
for its fruit is bitter on the day of enjoyment.

KURAL 178

To protect one's own prosperity from decline,
one must not crave the property held by others.

KURAL 179

Just as wise men know the goodness of noncoveting,
so Fortune Herself knows their goodness and draws near.

KURAL 180

There is a thoughtless desire for others' things that is destructive.
There is a mindful pride that, in refusing to covet, is triumphant.

புறங்கூறிப் பொய்த்துயிர் வாழ்தலின் சாதல்
அறங்கூறும் ஆக்கந் தரும்.

Avoidance of Backbiting

KURAL 181
Silent about virtue and swift to act wrongly,
one who does not slander others may still be called good.

KURAL 182
More vile than violating virtue and committing crime
is slandering a man, then smiling to his face.

KURAL 183
Virtue declares that dying, not living, will bring
better rewards to deceiving backbiters.

KURAL 184
Though you speak unkind words to a man's face,
do not talk behind his back heedless of consequent harm.

KURAL 185
Though his every word is full of kindly virtue,
a man's mean backbiting will betray an empty heart.

KURAL 186
If a man spreads tales of others' faults,
his own worst faults will be exposed and spread.

KURAL 187
Not knowing the companionable art of cheerful conversation,
men estrange even friends by divisive discourse.

KURAL 188
If men are disposed to spread the faults of friends,
what deadly harm might they do to strangers?

KURAL 189
Only because she weighs duty well does Earth bear the weight
of those who wait for a man's departure to defame him.

KURAL 190
If men perceived their own faults as they do the faults of others,
could misfortune ever come to them?

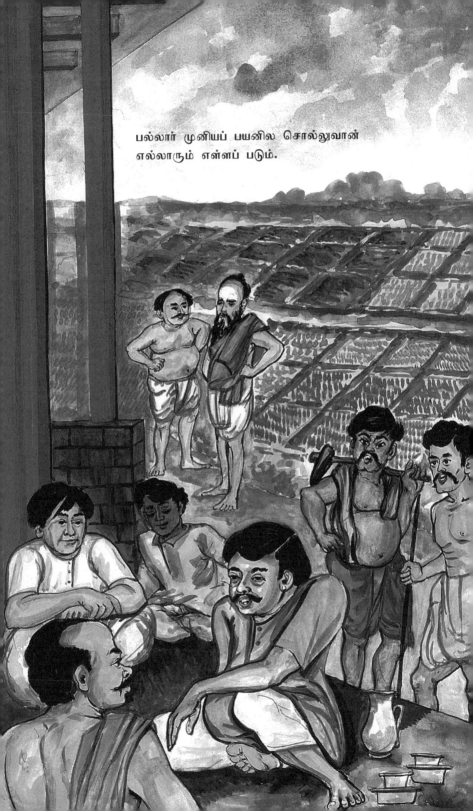

பல்லார் முனியப் பயனில சொல்லுவான்
எல்லாரும் எள்ளப் படும்.

Avoidance of Pointless Speech

KURAL 191

Everyone is disgusted by a man
who offends one and all with meaningless chatter.

KURAL 192

Uttering useless words to crowds is worse
than committing unkindnesses toward companions.

KURAL 193

A long and pointless discourse itself declares
to all the speaker's lack of worth.

KURAL 194

Worthless words are doubly unprofitable: the listeners'
enjoyment is lost, and the speaker's own virtues vanish.

KURAL 195

Prestige and popularity flee the best of men
the moment they speak inane and useless words.

KURAL 196

Do not call him a man who enjoys displaying
his own empty words. Rather, call him the chaff of men.

KURAL 197

Let the wise, if they deem it necessary, speak even unpleasant
words, but it is good if they always refrain from pointless speech.

KURAL 198

Even in search of extraordinary gains, the wise
will never speak trivial or ungainful words.

KURAL 199

The wise, faultless and free from ignorance,
never utter pointless words, even forgetfully.

KURAL 200

In your speaking, say only that which is purposeful.
Never utter words that lack purpose.

தீயவை செய்தார் கெடுதல் நிழல்தன்ஊ
வீயாது அடிஉறைந் தற்று.

Dread of Sinful Deeds

KURAL 201

Wicked men do not fear, but worthy men dread,
the arrogance of sinful deeds.

KURAL 202

From evil springs forth more evil.
Hence evil is to be feared even more than fire.

KURAL 203

To commit no wrong, even against one's enemies,
is said to be supreme wisdom.

KURAL 204

Only the forgetful plot another's ruin; others remember
that virtue itself devises every plotter's downfall.

KURAL 205

Do not commit wrongful deeds, claiming to be poor.
Such deeds only cause one to be poorer still.

KURAL 206

Let one who hopes for freedom from afflictions' pain
avoid inflicting harm on others.

KURAL 207

One can escape from hate-filled enemies,
but his own hateful acts will pursue and destroy him.

KURAL 208

As a man's shadow follows his footsteps wherever he goes,
even so will destruction pursue those who commit sinful deeds.

KURAL 209

If a man feels any fond affection for himself,
let him not indulge in immoral deeds, however trifling.

KURAL 210

If men neither deviate from right nor act wrongly,
they will be defended against destruction.

பயன்மரம் உள்ளூர்ப் பழுத்தற்றால் செல்வம்
நயனுடை யான்கண் படின்.

Understanding One's Duty to Give

KURAL 211

The benevolent expect no return for their dutiful giving.
How can the world ever repay the rain cloud?

KURAL 212

It is to meet the needs of the deserving
that the worthy work so hard to acquire wealth.

KURAL 213

Of all duties, none is better than benevolence,
whether in this world or that of the Gods.

KURAL 214

He who understands the duty of giving truly lives.
All others shall be counted among the dead.

KURAL 215

The wealth of a community-loving wise man
may be likened to a well-filled village water tank.

KURAL 216

Riches retained by the big-hearted resemble fruits
ripening on a tree in the heart of a village.

KURAL 217

In the hands of a generous man,
wealth is like a medicinal tree whose healing gifts help all.

KURAL 218

Those who know duty deeply never neglect giving,
even in their own unprosperous season.

KURAL 219

The benevolent man considers himself poor only
when he is unable to render his accustomed duty to humanity.

KURAL 220

Were it said that loss of wealth is the price of generosity,
such loss would be worth selling one's self to acquire.

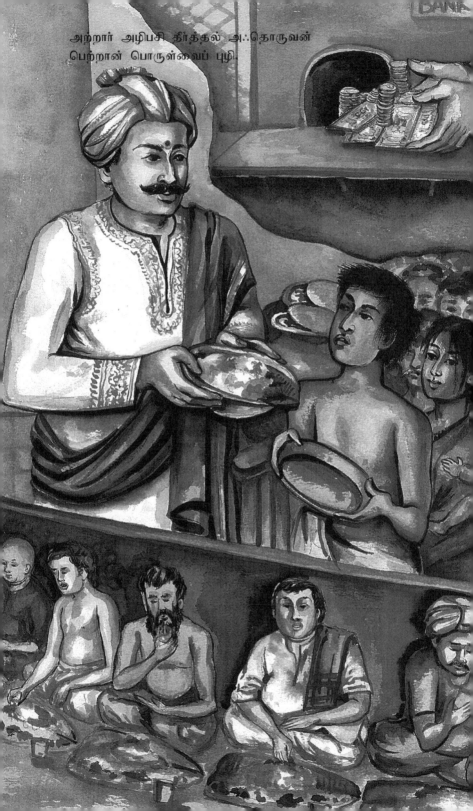

அற்றார் அழிபசி தீர்த்தல் அஃதொருவன்
பெற்றான் பொருள்வைப் புழி.

Charity

KURAL 221

Giving to the poor is true charity.
All other giving expects some return.

KURAL 222

Though some may declare it a good path, garnering gifts is bad.
Even if they say it denies one Heaven, giving gifts is good.

KURAL 223

Men of good birth graciously give,
never uttering the wretched excuse, "I have nothing."

KURAL 224

How unpleasant a beggar's pleading can become,
until one sees his face so sweetly pleased.

KURAL 225

Great, indeed, is the power to endure hunger.
Greater still is the power to relieve others' hunger.

KURAL 226

Relieving the ravaging hunger of the poor
is a right use for wealth men have obtained.

KURAL 227

The fiery scourge called hunger never touches
the man who shares his daily meal with others.

KURAL 228

Is it because they are unaware of the joys of giving
that hard-hearted men waste their wealth by hoarding it?

KURAL 229

More bitter than even a beggar's bread is the meal
of the miser who hoards wealth and eats alone.

KURAL 230

There is nothing more bitter than death;
yet even death seems sweet when giving is impossible.

வசையிலா வண்பயன் குன்றும் இசையிலா
யாக்கை பொறுத்த நிலம்.

Glory

KURAL 231

Give to the poor and become praiseworthy.
Life offers no greater reward than this.

KURAL 232

Those who expound will always praise
people who bestow alms on the imploring poor.

KURAL 233

Nothing on Earth is imperishable,
except exalted glory, which endures forever.

KURAL 234

So great is glory gained by men in this world
that celestials cease praising ascended sages.

KURAL 235

Loss that is gain and death that is life of
immortal glory are attained only by the wise.

KURAL 236

If you must be born, be born for glory.
Those born without it would be better off without birth.

KURAL 237

Why do those whose life is devoid of renown blame enemies
who hate them, when they have themselves to blame?

KURAL 238

Barren are they and deemed a disgrace by all men on Earth
who fail to beget the offspring called fame.

KURAL 239

Even flawlessly fruitful lands will lessen their yields
when forced to support the body of one who lacks illustriousness.

KURAL 240

Those who live without reproach truly live.
Those who live without renown don't live at all.

Turavaraviyal
துறவறவியல்

உற்றநோய் நோன்றல் உயிர்க்குறுகண் செய்யாமை
அற்றே தவத்திற் குரு.

Section III
The Way of
The Renunciate

KURAL 261
It is the nature of asceticism to patiently endure hardship
and to not harm living creatures.

THE IDEAL FOLLOWED BY THE RENUNCIATE IS ELUCI-
DATED IN THIS SECTION OF *WEAVER'S WISDOM.* IN
THE WEAVER'S DAY, LONG AGO, AS IT IS TODAY, THE
two paths—that of the family and that of the renunciate—
were and are the core of society. In India today, millions pilgrimage to the great festivals called *kumbhamela,* where the
two paths meet for a few months every three years. Thousands of renunciates teach and preach in tents to millions of
seekers. In the nine chapters here are found the essential
teachings to be passed on by the ministers of the religion to
their followers, especially by example, for it is the renunciates
who can live these truths most fully and constantly. Householders can only try. There is one hope in every devout Hindu's heart: that each elderly father, having raised his family
well, will retire in his later years and join the band of renunciates, to perform penance and make ready for yet another
life, when he may take up the highest path, that of the renunciate, which Valluvar calls by the sweet Tamil name, *thuravi.*

The eminent Swami Vivekananda defined this path so eloquently in his never-to-be-forgotten poem, "Song of the Sannyasin." When I was a young man, this poem moved me,
brought before my vision the Great Path of the Hindu monk
and world-renouncer, led me at an early age to give up the
world and seek God, just as many in the weaver's time were
so inspired. Fifty years earlier, my spiritual preceptor, Satguru Yogaswami of Jaffna, Sri Lanka, stood in a festive crowd as
Swami Vivekananda was paraded through Jaffna on his return to India from America. The young Tamil man, later to become the greatest sage of the 20th century, was also moved by
Swami Vivekananda's living example to choose the path of
the renunciate. I commend Vivekananda's poem to all who
wish to know the spirit of the path that leads to liberation
from rebirth, the path known and valued in Valluvar's day as
one-half of dharma's fulfillment.

Song of the Sannyasin

Wake up the note! the song that had its birth
Far off, where worldly taint could never reach,
In mountain caves and glades of forest deep,
Whose calm no sigh for lust or wealth or fame
Could ever dare to break; where rolled the stream
Of knowledge, truth, and bliss that follows both.
Sing high that note, *sannyasin* bold! Say,
"Om Tat Sat, Om!"

Strike off thy fetters! bonds that bind thee down,
Of shining gold, or darker, baser ore—
Love, hate; good, bad; and all the dual throng.
Know slave is slave, caressed or whipped, not free;
For fetters, though of gold, are not less strong to bind.
Then off with them, *sannyasin* bold! Say,
"Om Tat Sat, Om!"

Let darkness go; the will-o'-the-wisp that leads
With blinking light to pile more gloom on gloom.
This thirst for life forever quench; it drags
From birth to death, and death to birth, the soul.
He conquers all who conquers self.
Know this and never yield, *sannyasin* bold! Say,
"Om Tat Sat, Om!"

"Who sows must reap," they say, "and cause must bring
The sure effect: good, good; bad, bad; and none
Escapes the law. But whoso wears a form
Must wear the chain." Too true; but far beyond
Both name and form is *atman*, ever free.
Know thou art That, *sannyasin* bold! Say,
"Om Tat Sat, Om!"

They know not truth who dream such vacant dreams
As father, mother, children, wife and friend.
The sexless Self—whose father He? whose child?
Whose friend, whose foe, is He who is but One?
The Self is all in all—none else exists;
And thou art That, *sannyasin* bold! Say,
"Om Tat Sat, Om!"

There is but One: the Free, the Knower, Self,
Without a name, without a form or stain.
In Him is *maya*, dreaming all this dream.
The Witness, He appears as nature, soul.
Know thou art That, *sannyasin* bold! Say,
"Om Tat Sat, Om!"

Where seekest thou? That freedom, friend, this world
Nor that can give. In books and temples, vain
Thy search. Thine only is the hand that holds
The rope that drags thee on. Then cease lament.
Let go thy hold, *sannyasin* bold! Say,
"Om Tat Sat, Om!"

Say, "Peace to all. From me no danger be
To aught that lives. In those that dwell on high,
In those that lowly creep—I am the Self in all!
All life, both here and there, do I renounce,
All heavens and earths and hells, all hopes and fears."
Thus cut thy bonds, *sannyasin* bold! Say,
"Om Tat Sat, Om!"

Heed then no more how body lives or goes.
Its task is done: let karma float it down.
Let one put garlands on, another kick
This frame: say naught. No praise or blame can be
Where praiser, praised, and blamer, blamed, are one.
Thus be thou calm, *sannyasin* bold! Say,
"Om Tat Sat, Om!"

Truth never comes where lust and fame and greed
Of gain reside. No man who thinks of woman
As his wife can ever perfect be;
Nor he who owns the least of things, nor he
Whom anger Chains, can ever pass through *maya's* gates.
So, give these up, *sannyasin* bold! Say,
"Om Tat Sat, Om!"

Have thou no home. What home can hold thee, friend?
The sky thy roof, the grass thy bed, and food
What chance may bring—well cooked or ill, judge not.
No food or drink can taint that noble Self
Which knows Itself. Like rolling river free
Thou ever be, *sannyasin* bold! Say,
"Om Tat Sat, Om!"

Few only know the truth. The rest will hate
And laugh at thee, great one; but pay no heed.
Go thou, the free, from place to place, and help
Them out of darkness, *maya's* veil. Without
The fear of pain or search for pleasure, go
Beyond them both, *sannyasin* bold! Say,
"Om Tat Sat, Om!"

Thus day by day, till karma's power's spent,
Release the soul forever. No more is birth,
Nor I, nor thou, nor God, nor man. The "I"
Has All become, the All is "I" and Bliss.
Know thou art That, *sannyasin* bold! Say,
"Om Tat Sat, Om!"

"Song of the Sannyasin" by Swami Vivekananda is quoted, with written permission, from *Inspired Talks, My Master and Other Writings*; copyright 1958 by Swami Nikhilananda, trustee of the estate of Swami Vivekananda; published by the Ramakrishna-Vivekananda Center of New York. Remarkably, the handwritten original was discovered (long after his passing in 1902) hidden in a wall during the 1943 restoration of a retreat where Swamiji had spent the summer and given *darshan* and discourses to Western seekers.

வலியார்முன் தன்னை நினைக்கதான் தன்னின்
மெலியார்மேல் செல்லும் இடத்து.

Possession of Compassion

KURAL 241

Among the wealthy, compassionate men claim the richest wealth,
for material wealth is possessed even by contemptible men.

KURAL 242

Find and follow the good path, ruled by compassion.
Of the many ways, that one leads to liberation.

KURAL 243

Those whose hearts are drawn toward mercy
will never be drawn into the dark and woeful world.

KURAL 244

Kindly ones who lovingly protect all life
need never dread hurt from the actions of their own life.

KURAL 245

This wide and wind-swept fertile Earth is witness to the truth
that misery is not for kind-hearted men.

KURAL 246

They say those who act cruelly by forsaking kindness
must have forgotten what it means to forsake virtue.

KURAL 247

As this world is not for the penniless,
so is that world not for the pitiless!

KURAL 248

Those without wealth may one day prosper,
but those without kindness are utterly and incurably poor.

KURAL 249

Practicing charity without compassion is as inconceivable
as realizing God without clarity of mind.

KURAL 250

Before proceeding against men weaker than yourself,
ponder when you stood before those more powerful.

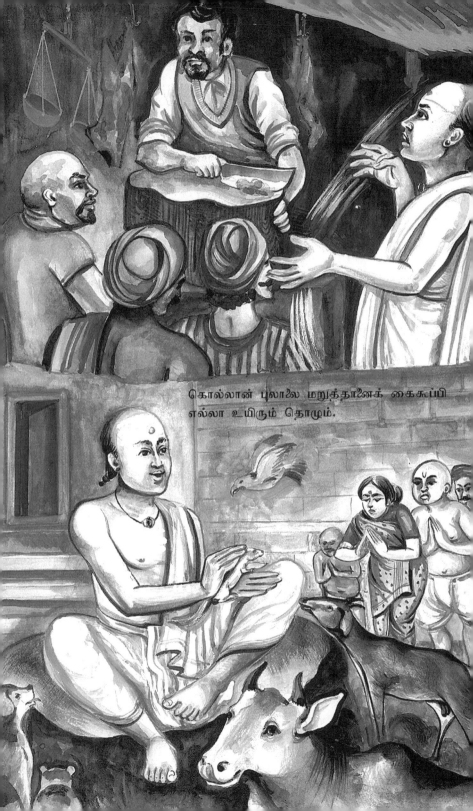

கொல்லான் புலாலை மறுத்தானைக் கைகூப்பி
எல்லா உயிரும் தொழும்.

Abstaining from Eating Meat

KURAL 251

How can he practice true compassion
who eats the flesh of an animal to fatten his own flesh?

KURAL 252

Riches cannot be found in the hands of the thriftless,
nor can compassion be found in the hearts of those who eat meat.

KURAL 253

He who feasts on a creature's flesh is like he who wields a weapon.
Goodness is never one with the minds of these two.

KURAL 254

If you ask, "What is kindness and what is unkindness?"
It is not-killing and killing. Thus, eating flesh is never virtuous.

KURAL255

Life is perpetuated by not eating meat.
The jaws of Hell close on those who do.

KURAL 256

If the world did not purchase and consume meat,
no one would slaughter and offer meat for sale.

KURAL 257

When a man realizes that meat is the butchered flesh
of another creature, he will abstain from eating it.

KURAL 258

Insightful souls who have abandoned the passion to hurt others
will not feed on flesh that life has abandoned.

KURAL 259

Greater than a thousand ghee offerings consumed in sacrificial
fires is to not sacrifice and consume any living creature.

KURAL 260

All life will press palms together in prayerful adoration
of those who refuse to slaughter or savor meat.

சுடச்சுடரும் பொன்போல் ஒளிவிடும் துன்பஞ்
சுடச்சுட நோற்கிற் பவர்க்கு.

Austerity

KURAL 261
It is the nature of asceticism to patiently endure hardship
and to not harm living creatures.

KURAL 262
Austerity belongs to the naturally austere.
Others may attempt it, but to no avail.

KURAL 263
Is it because they must provide for renunciates
that others forget to perform penance?

KURAL 264
Should he but wish it, an ascetic's austerities
will ruin his foes and reward his friends.

KURAL 265
In this world men do austerities diligently,
assured of acquiring desires they desire.

KURAL 266
Men who follow some austerity fulfill their karma.
All others, ensnared in desires, act in vain.

KURAL 267
As the intense fire of the furnace refines gold to brilliance, so does
the burning suffering of austerity purify the soul to resplendence.

KURAL 268
One who has realized by himself his soul's Self
will be worshiped by all other souls.

KURAL 269
So potent is the power acquired through disciplined self-denial
that those who attain it may even delay the moment of death.

KURAL 270
A few people fast and abstain, while most do not.
Due to this, many suffer deprivation.

மனத்தது மாசாக மாண்டார் நீராடி
மறைந்தொழுகு மாந்தர் பலர்.

Deceptive Conduct

KURAL 271

A deceiver's own five elements remain undeceived
by his double-dealing mind and silently mock him.

KURAL 272

Of what avail is an outer appearance of saintliness
if the mind suffers inwardly from knowledge of its iniquity?

KURAL 273

He who has not attained the power yet wears the garb of saints
is like a cow that grazes about wearing a tiger's skin.

KURAL 274

He who conceals himself beneath holy robes and commits sins
is like a hunter hiding in the bushes to snare unwary birds.

KURAL 275

The day will come when those who claim dispassion
yet act deceitfully exclaim,"Alas! Alas! What have I done?"

KURAL 276

None is so heartless as he who, without renunciation in his heart,
poses as a renunciate and lives in pretense.

KURAL 277

Like the poisonous jequirity bean, with its red and black sides,
there are outwardly dazzling men whose insides are dark.

KURAL 278

Many are the men who piously bathe in purifying waters,
while in their black hearts impure conduct lies concealed.

KURAL 279

The arrow is straight but cruel; the lute is crooked but sweet.
Therefore, judge men by their acts, not their appearance.

KURAL 280

Neither shaven head nor long matted locks are needed,
provided one casts off conduct condemned by the world.

களவினால் ஆகிய ஆக்கம் அளவிறந்து
ஆவது போலக் கெடும்.

Avoidance of Fraud

KURAL 281

He who wishes not to be scorned by others
guards his own mind against the slightest thought of fraud.

KURAL 282

The mere thought of sin is sin. Therefore,
avoid even the thought of stealing from another.

KURAL 283

A fortune amassed by fraud may appear to prosper
but will all too soon perish altogether.

KURAL 284

Taking delight in defrauding others yields the fruit
of undying suffering when those delights ripen.

KURAL 285

Benevolent thoughts and kindly feelings flee from those
who watch for another's unwatchfulness to swindle his property.

KURAL 286

Those who walk deceit's desirous path
cannot hope to work wisdom's measured way.

KURAL 287

The dark deceits of fraud cannot be found
in those who desire the greatness called virtue.

KURAL 288

As righteousness resides in the hearts of the virtuous,
so does deceit dwell in the hearts of thieves.

KURAL 289

Men who know nothing but deception die a little
each time they contrive their crooked deeds.

KURAL 290

Even the life in his body will abandon him who cheats others,
while Heaven itself never forsakes those who are honest.

எல்லா விளக்கும் விளக்கல்ல சான்றோர்க்குப்
பொய்யா விளக்கே விளக்கு.

Truthfulness

KURAL 291

What is truthfulness? It is speaking words
which are totally free from harmful effects.

KURAL 292

Even falsehood is of the nature of truth
if it renders good results, free from fault.

KURAL 293

Let one not speak as true what he knows to be false,
for his conscience will burn him when he has lied.

KURAL 294

One who lives by truth in his own heart
truly lives in the hearts of all people.

KURAL 295

Those who speak only truth from the heart
surpass even penitents and philanthropists.

KURAL 296

No prestige surpasses the absence of falsehood;
all other virtues flow from it effortlessly.

KURAL 297

Not lying, and merely not lying, is beneficial
for those who cannot or will not practice other virtues.

KURAL 298

Water is sufficient to cleanse the body,
but truthfulness alone can purify the mind.

KURAL 299

Not all lamps give light.
The lamp of not-lying is the learned man's light.

KURAL 300

Among all great truths we have ever beheld,
not a single one rivals the goodness of telling the truth.

சினமென்னும் சேர்ந்தாரைக் கொல்லி இனமென்னும்
ஏமப் புணையைச் சுடும்.

Avoidance of Anger

KURAL 301

It is restraint that restrains rage when it can injure.
If it cannot harm, what does restraint really matter?

KURAL 302

Wrath is wrong even when it cannot cause injury,
but when it can, there is nothing more evil.

KURAL 303

Forget anger toward all who have offended you,
for it gives rise to teeming troubles.

KURAL 304

Anger kills the face's smile and the heart's joy.
Does there exist a greater enemy than one's own anger?

KURAL 305

If a man be his own guard, let him guard himself against rage.
Left unguarded, his own wrath will annihilate him.

KURAL 306

Anger's fire engulfs all who draw near it,
burning even friends and family who risk rescue.

KURAL 307

As a man trying to strike the ground with his hand can hardly fail,
just as surely will one who treasures his temper be destroyed.

KURAL 308

Though others inflict wrongs as painful as flaming torches,
it is good if a man can refrain from inflammatory tantrums.

KURAL 309

If hostile thoughts do not invade his mind,
all his other thoughts may swiftly manifest.

KURAL 310

As men who have died resemble the dead,
so men who have renounced rage resemble renunciates.

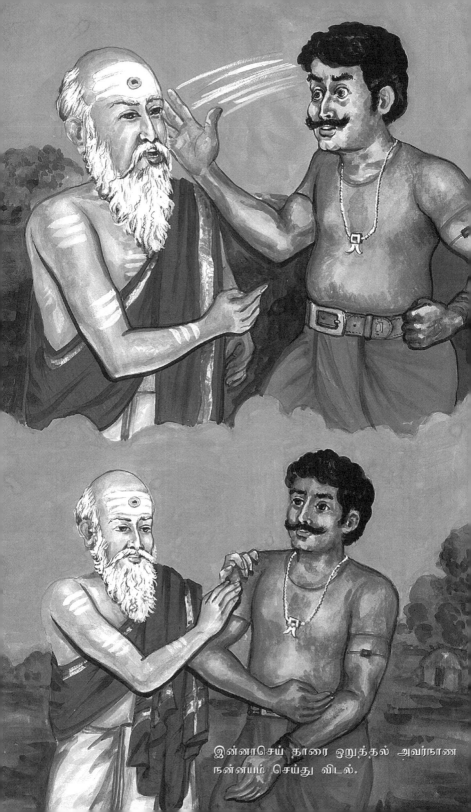

இன்னாசெய் தாரை ஒறுத்தல் அவர்நாண
நன்னயம் செய்து விடல்.

Avoidance of Injuring Others

KURAL 311
Even if injuring others would bring princely riches,
the pure in heart would still avoid it.

KURAL 312
It is the principle of the pure in heart never to injure others,
even when they themselves have been hatefully injured.

KURAL 313
Harming others, even enemies who harmed you unprovoked,
surely brings incessant sorrow.

KURAL 314
If you return kindness for injuries received and forget both,
Those who harmed you will be punished by their own shame.

KURAL 315
What good is a man's knowledge unless it prompts him
to prevent the pain of others as if it were his own pain?

KURAL 316
Actions that are known to harm oneself
should never be inflicted upon others.

KURAL 317
The highest principle is this: never knowingly
harm anyone at any time in any way.

KURAL 318
Why does he who knows what injury to his own life is like
inflict injury upon other living human beings?

KURAL 319
If a man visits sorrow on another in the morning,
sorrow will visit him unbidden in the afternoon.

KURAL 320
All suffering recoils on the wrongdoer himself. Thus, those
desiring not to suffer refrain from causing others pain.

கொல்லாமை மேற்கொண் டொழுகுவான் வாழ்நாள்மேல்
செல்லாது உயிருண்ணுங் கூற்று.

Avoidance of Killing

KURAL 321

What is virtuous conduct? It is never destroying life,
for killing leads to every other sin.

KURAL 322

Of all virtues summed by ancient sages, the foremost are to
share one's food and to protect all living creatures.

KURAL 323

Not killing is the first and foremost good.
The virtue of not lying comes next.

KURAL 324

What is the good way? It is the path that reflects on
how it may avoid killing any living creature.

KURAL 325

Among all who disown the world out of dismay,
the foremost, dismayed with killing, embrace nonkilling.

KURAL 326

Life-devouring death will not lay waste the living days
of one whose code of conduct is to never kill.

KURAL 327

Refrain from taking precious life from any living being,
even to save your own life.

KURAL 328

By sacrifice of life, some gain great wealth and welfare,
but great men scorn such odious gains.

KURAL 329

Those whose trade is killing creatures are deemed defiled
by men who know the defiling nature of being mean.

KURAL 330

They say that beggars who suffer a depraved life
in a diseased body once deprived another's body of its life.

நில்லாத வற்றை நிலேயின என்றுணரும்
புல்லறி வாண்மை கடை.

Impermanence of All Things

KURAL 331

There is no baser folly than the infatuation
that looks upon the ephemeral as if it were everlasting.

KURAL 332

Amassing great wealth is gradual, like the gathering of a theater
crowd. Its dispersal is sudden, like that same crowd departing.

KURAL 333

Wealth's nature is to be unenduring.
Upon acquiring it, quickly do that which is enduring.

KURAL 334

Though it seems a harmless gauge of time, to those who fathom it,
a day is a saw steadily cutting down the tree of life.

KURAL 335

Do good deeds with a sense of urgency,
before death's approaching rattle strangles the tongue.

KURAL 336

What wondrous greatness this world possesses—
that yesterday a man was, and today he is not.

KURAL 337

Men do not know if they will live another moment,
yet their thoughts are ten million and more.

KURAL 338

The soul's attachment to the body is like that of a fledgling,
which forsakes its empty shell and flies away.

KURAL 339

Death is like falling asleep,
and birth is like waking from that sleep.

KURAL 340

Not yet settled in a permanent home,
the soul takes temporary shelter in a body.

பற்றுக பற்றற்றான் பற்றினை அப்பற்றைப்
பற்றுக பற்று விடற்கு.

Renunciation

KURAL 341

Whatsoever a man has renounced,
from the sorrow born of that he has freed himself.

KURAL 342

The greatest gladness in the world comes after renunciation.
Let men desiring that rapture renounce early in life.

KURAL 343

The five senses must be subdued,
and every desire simultaneously surrendered.

KURAL 344

The ascetic's austerity permits not a single possession,
for possessions draw him back into delusion.

KURAL 345

What are life's petty attachments to the man who seeks severance
from future births, when even his body is a burden?

KURAL 346

One who slays the conceit that clamors "I" and "mine"
will reach a realm above the celestials' world.

KURAL 347

If one clings to his attachments, refusing to let go,
sorrows will not let go their grip on him.

KURAL 348

Those who perfectly renounce attain the highest peak;
the rest remain ensnared in delusion's net.

KURAL 349

Birth ceases when all attachments are severed;
until then, one only sees life's impermanence.

KURAL 350

Attach yourself to Him who is free from all attachments.
Bind yourself to that bond so all other bonds may be broken.

பிறப்பென்னும் பேதைமை நீங்கச் சிறப்பென்னும்
செம்பொருள் காண்பது அறிவு.

Knowledge of Truth

KURAL 351

The muddled mentality that mistakes the unreal for the Real
is the genesis of woeful births.

KURAL 352

For those of undimmed perception, free from delusion,
darkness departs and rapture rushes in.

KURAL 353

Heaven is nearer than Earth for those who
dispel all doubt and know the Truth.

KURAL 354

All knowledge acquired through the five senses is worthless
to those without knowledge of Truth.

KURAL 355

In everything of every kind whatsoever,
wisdom perceives Truth in that thing.

KURAL 356

Those who find the highest Reality here and now
follow a path which never comes back to this world.

KURAL 357

Having thought profoundly and realized fully That which is,
one need never think of being born again.

KURAL 358

Wisdom is that rare realization of Perfection's True Being,
which banishes forever the folly of rebirth.

KURAL 359

He who clings to life's true support clings not to lesser things.
Sorrows, which destroy by clinging, no longer cling to him.

KURAL 360

Desire, delusion and indignation—annihilation of these
three terms is the termination of torment.

ஆரா இயற்கை அவாங்கிப்பின் அங்கினிலயே
பேரா இயற்கை தரும்.

Eradication of Desire

KURAL 361

At all times and to all creatures,
the seed of ceaseless births is desire.

KURAL 362

If you must desire, desire freedom from birth.
That will only come by desiring desirelessness.

KURAL 363

Here no fortune is as dear as desirelessness;
and even there, nothing like it can be found.

KURAL 364

Purity is but freedom from desire,
and that comes from thirsting after Truth.

KURAL 365

They say only those who have renounced desire are renunciates.
Others, though they have renounced all else, are not.

KURAL 366

As it is desire, above all else, which deceives a man,
ascetics rightfully dread it.

KURAL 367

Desisting from all desire-driven deeds, a renouncer
finds liberation approaching, just as he desired.

KURAL 368

He who has no desires has no sorrow.
But where desire exists, endless sorrows ensue.

KURAL 369

When desire, sorrow's sorrow, dies away,
undying bliss prevails here on Earth.

KURAL 370

It is the nature of desire never to be fulfilled, but he who utterly
gives it up is eternally fulfilled at that very moment.

Uull
உழ்

Section IV
Destiny

KURAL 376

Though you guard it well, what destiny does not decree disappears.
Though you cast it aside, what destiny calls yours will not depart.

AH! DESTINY. SOMETHING THAT APPLIES TO BOTH
PATHS: THAT OF THE FAMILIES AND THAT OF THE
RENUNCIATES. CALL IT KARMA, BUT NEVER FATE.
Some have translated the Tamil word *uull* as fate, equating
fate with karma. However, *fate* implies an unavoidable doom,
and that is not a description of karma. *Webster's Dictionary*
says, "*Fate* refers to the inevitability of a course of events as
supposedly predetermined by a God or other agency beyond
human control. *Destiny* refers to an inevitable succession of
events as determined supernaturally or by necessity, but often
implies a favorable outcome." I prefer the word *destiny*—from
the Latin, meaning "determination," "fixed standing"—if either must be used, as it implies less inevitability and flows
better with the reality that each soul creates its own future
by its own actions.

Fortunately, in recent times, the word *karma* has been
brought into English. *Webster's* defines it as, "A deed, act, fate.
To make, form. Similar to the Welsh *pryd:* shape, time. 1) Hinduism, Buddhism: the totality of a person's actions in any one
of the successive states of that person's existence, thought of
as determining the fate of the next stage. 2) Loosely, fate, destiny." This reveals a combination of destiny, fate and karma to
unfold the complexity of how the soul shapes its own future.

It is interesting to note that the originally Latin word *fate*
("pronouncement, prediction, prophecy") actually goes back to
the times of the Greeks and Romans, when the Fates, as they
were called (also Moirai for the Greeks and Parcae for the Romans), were three Goddesses—Clotho, Lachesis and Atropos—
believed to guide human destiny. We might surmise that their
role was or is like that of guardian *devas,* or even Mahadevas,
who assist man in shaping his own destiny by revealing path-
ways that are auspicious and karmically positive. The Greeks
say that Clotho is the spinner of the thread of destiny. Lachesis
is the measurer of the thread of destiny. Atropos is the cutter

of the fabric of destiny.

I have never liked the word *fate*. It has always reminded me of the strain of fatalism in the Abrahamic religions, preaching that everything is predetermined, foreordained, and there is nothing you can do if you are doomed. You are at the mercy of outside, and sometimes hurtful, forces. The burden is intolerable, in spite of some theologians' efforts to alleviate it by elaboration of the concept of free will. The Vedic traditional view of karma is not of this kind. *Jyotisha*, Hindu astrology, tells us the stars only impel; they do not compel. Karmas are of man's own making, making him the creator of his own destiny, not the victim of some other force, whether divine or not. Bad karmas (*kukarma* in Sanskrit) can be mitigated through remorse, prayer and penance, called *prayashchitta*. Though karmas may be the worst of the worst, once they are mitigated and atoned for, one can lead a joyous, happy religious life.

Fate, on the other hand, is taken as a damnation, a curse from God if it is bad, and nothing, literally nothing, can be done to soften or avoid it. The concept of fate holds one who believes in it in a state of constant, ever-growing fear and hopelessness. Fate is a foreordained destiny imposed upon each person from some unseen outside force, whereas karma is of man's own making. As we explain in *Dancing with Siva*, "Karma is not fate, for man acts with free will, creating his own destiny. The *Vedas* tell us, if we sow goodness, we will reap goodness; if we sow evil, we will reap evil. Karma refers to the totality of our actions and their concomitant reactions in this and previous lives, all of which determines our future. It is the interplay between our experience and how we respond to it that makes karma devastating or helpfully invigorating."

வீகுத்தான் வீகுத்த வகையல்லால் கோடி
தொகுத்தார்க்குத் துய்த்தல் அரிது.

Destiny

KURAL 371

When destiny ordains wealth, it gives birth to industriousness.
When it decrees a life of loss, it inspires only idleness.

KURAL 372

That destiny which decreases prosperity increases ignorance.
That destiny which diminishes loss expands knowledge.

KURAL 373

However subtle the sundry texts he studies,
a man is left with his native intelligence.

KURAL 374

Two natural ways are ordained in this world.
Securing wealth is one. Seeking wisdom's light is another.

KURAL 375

In karma's presence, sure success with wealth can fail,
and certain failure can succeed.

KURAL 376

Though you guard it well, what destiny does not decree disappears.
Though you cast it aside, what destiny calls yours will not depart.

KURAL 377

A man may amass millions, but its enjoyment
will never exceed the portion allotted to him.

KURAL 378

The poor are practically ascetics and would renounce if only karma,
approaching with experiences yet to be, would pass them by.

KURAL 379

Why should those who rejoice when destiny brings them good
moan when that same destiny decrees misfortune?

KURAL 380

What is there that is mightier than destiny?
For it is present even in the plans we devise to overcome it.

Porutpaal

பொருட்பால்

Part II

On Wealth

Arasiyal
அரசியல்

கொடையளி செங்கோல் குடியோம்பல் நான்கும்
உடையானாம் வெந்தர்க் கொளி.

Section V
Royalty

KURAL 390
He is a light among rulers who is endowed with the four merits
of generosity, graciousness, justice and care for the people.

Y ES, THERE ARE SO FEW KINGS LEFT ON OUR PLANET
TODAY, BUT THEY ARE STILL HERE, AND THIS SEC-
TION ON GOVERNMENT APPLIES TO THEM. BUT DOES
it apply to them only? Is it not a course in human resource
management, essential for all who aspire to climb the corporate ladder? Is it not a politician's handbook for those who aspire to the top and wish to remain there? In today's world, the
CEOs of large corporations far outnumber even the subjects of
feudal kingdoms of the days in which Valluvar lived. Earth's
population then was only 150 million or more, and now it is
nearly six billion—forty times greater.

Here we learn that right thought, right speech and right action are a total must for right government for the corporation,
the political arena, for a president of a large or small nation,
or for a king. Indeed, these precepts apply to all of us who aspire to serve without conflict, to think ahead and prepare, to
analyze and understand before we act. It is all here: an ir-
refutable and clear message for success.

There is no way to calculate how many Hindus have memorized and acted upon these verses and are now top in the
computer industries, leaders in political circles, directors of
hospitals or highly regarded engineers within their fields.
Take, for example, the admonitions on choosing the right people to employ, to associate with and to trust. This is wisdom
that needs to be known. Certain men who commanded high
esteem failed to comply with what is so clearly outlined here,
and the thud of their fall was heard worldwide through the
Internet, the television, the radio and the printed word. For
this alone, *Weaver's Wisdom* is a must, for it is with great effort that one attains to a position of worth, and it is by even
greater effort that he maintains this position to fulfill the ini-
tial vision of his chosen enterprise. It is for this that information "spies" are needed, that loyal and trusted advisors are
needed, that wealth obtained by proper means is needed, that

fairness to employees, constituents and the public at large is needed, and most of all the knowledge of exactly what fairness actually is, so as not to earn reproach.

Valluvar explains how to learn and the importance of learning. He states that life is a continuum of constant learning, keeping up with the times. In today's world, the times are moving rapidly, and there is a lot of keeping up to do. For leaders, it is a constant demand. The weaver admonishes those who neglect their learning, who are too indolent to tolerate a new idea, absorb a new duty or take on a new responsibility. Skillfully, he divides the intellectual from the wise in chapter 43, for wisdom is the timely application of knowledge. Self-reflection is seen in chapter 44, where the weaver explains that we must be self-reflective, see our own faults and correct them before others see them and complain—a hallmark of good leadership.

We can do nothing on the way up the corporate ladder, or even beginning a political campaign, unless we gain the support of those in influence. It is in chapter 45 that the weaver explains how this is done and the necessity for it. Yes, of course, there are admonitions that leaders will fall by not following, such as the wisdom that not avoiding low-minded people leads to ruin. Where would CNN, Doordarshan and other news media such as *India Today*, *Newsweek*, *The Hindu* and *Wall Street Journal* get their stories and their readership if all those in powerful positions heeded this chapter?

On and on he goes in creating the eminent management manual of all times, so precise are his statements, so true and so meaningful. He encourages all to persevere: "Laugh when troubles come your way. Nothing conquers calamity better than that."

முறைசெய்து காப்பாற்றும்
மன்னவன் மக்கட்கு
இறையென்று வைக்கப் படும்.

The Merits of the King

KURAL 381
He is lion among kings who is well endowed with these six:
army, citizens, wealth, ministers, allies and fortresses.

KURAL 382
There are four attributes that cannot be absent in a king:
fearlessness, generosity, wisdom and industriousness.

KURAL 383
In those who rule the land, three traits must never lapse:
vigilance, valor and virtuous learning.

KURAL 384
The noble king is unswerving in virtue, restrains wrongdoing
and courageously maintains his honor.

KURAL 385
He who can produce a treasury of wealth, deposit it,
preserve it and apportion it wisely—now, that is a king!

KURAL 386
All peoples praise that nation whose sovereign
is always accessible and never speaks harshly.

KURAL 387
Behold the king who speaks graciously, gives generously and
protects powerfully—the world considers his word its command.

KURAL 388
Ruling righteously himself and safeguarding his subjects,
a monarch may be deemed divine by his people.

KURAL 389
The world lives protected beneath the umbrella
of an ethical leader who can endure words bitter to the ear.

KURAL 390
He is a light among rulers who is endowed with the four merits
of generosity, graciousness, justice and care for the people.

எண்ணென்ப ஏனை எழுத்தென்ப இவ்விரண்டும்
கண்ணென்ப வாழும் உயிர்க்கு.

Learning

KURAL 391

All that you learn, learn perfectly, and
thereafter keep your conduct worthy of that learning.

KURAL 392

Two are the eyes of those who truly live—
one is called numbers, and the other letters.

KURAL 393

The learned have eyes that see, they say.
The unlearned have two open sores on their face.

KURAL 394

It is the learned man's prowess that meetings with him
bring delight, and departures leave pleasant thoughts.

KURAL 395

The learned remain ever humble, as the poor are before
the prosperous. Lowly men lack such learning.

KURAL 396

The deeper a sand well is dug, the more freely its water flows.
Even so, the deeper a man's learning, the greater is his wisdom.

KURAL 397

Knowing that knowledge makes all nations and neighborhoods
one's own, how can a man stay untutored until his death?

KURAL 398

The learning a man secures in one birth
will secure his well-being in seven.

KURAL 399

When the learned discern that the learning which delights them
also delights the world, they love learning all the more.

KURAL 400

A man's learning is an imperishable and precious wealth.
No other possession is as golden.

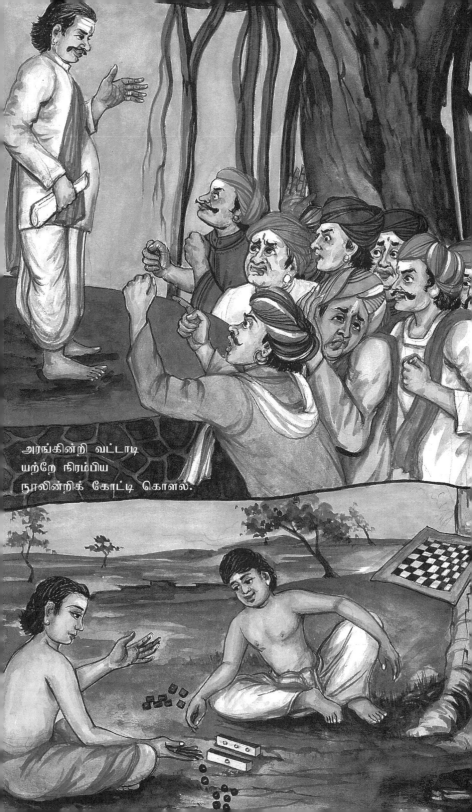

அரங்கின்றி வட்டாடி
யற்றே நிரம்பிய
நூலின்றிக் கோட்டி கொளல்.

The Neglect of Learning

KURAL 401

Speaking to a learned gathering without ample knowledge
is like playing a dice game without the board.

KURAL 402

An uneducated man desiring to be eloquent
is like a breastless woman longing to be feminine.

KURAL 403

Even the ignorant will be considered wise
if they refrain from speaking in the presence of the learned.

KURAL 404

However excellent an untaught man's knowledge may be,
erudite men will never accept it.

KURAL 405

An unschooled man's self-conceit will shrivel
the moment he speaks to an assembly.

KURAL 406

Like unproductive barren land is the man who has neglected
learning. All that can be said about him is that he exists.

KURAL 407

The handsome charm of him whose knowledge
is neither subtle nor penetrating is like that of a painted clay doll.

KURAL 408

Even more wretched than a learned man's poverty
is the unlearned man's wealth.

KURAL 409

Though he is humbly born, a lettered man's nobility
transcends that of the illiterate nobleman.

KURAL 410

As men are to wild beasts, so are the masters
of brilliant texts to other men.

இழுக்கல் உடையுழி ஊற்றுக்கோலல அற்றே
ஒழுக்க முடையார்வாய்ச் சொல்.

Learning by Listening

KURAL 411

The most precious wealth is the wealth acquired by the ear.
Indeed, of all wealth, that wealth is paramount.

KURAL 412

Only when no fare can be found for the ear
is it time to offer the stomach a morsel.

KURAL 413

In Heaven, Deities feed from sacrificial fires.
On Earth, men who feast on listening are their equal.

KURAL 414

Though he has no learning, if a man listens to the learned,
that will serve as his staff of strength in adversity.

KURAL 415

Words from the lips of upright men
are like a steadying staff in a slippery place.

KURAL 416

Let a man listen to good things, however little.
Even that little will enlarge his greatness.

KURAL 417

Those who have studied deeply and listened diligently never speak
foolish words, even when they have misunderstood a matter.

KURAL 418

If not pierced by acute listening,
ears may hear and yet remain deaf.

KURAL 419

Unless he has listened to learning's subtlety,
it is rare indeed for a man to speak with humility.

KURAL 420

There are those whose tongues taste but whose ears savor nothing.
What does it matter whether they live or die?

உலகம் தழீஇய தொட்பம் மலர்தலும்
கூம்பலும் இல்ல தறிவு.

Possession of Wisdom

KURAL 421

Wisdom is a weapon that can ward off destruction.
It is an inner fortress that no enemy can assail.

KURAL 422

Wisdom will harness the mind, diverting it
from wrong and directing it toward right.

KURAL 423

Whatever is heard from whomever's lips,
wisdom will rightly discern its true meaning.

KURAL 424

Wisdom speaks well, conveying each meaning clearly,
and listens for the subtlest sense in others' speech.

KURAL 425

The wise befriend the wise and keep that friendship constant,
not opening and closing it like the petaled lotus.

KURAL 426

It is wisdom to live in the world
in the way that the world lives.

KURAL 427

Those who know, know what will happen next.
Such things are unknown to the unknowing.

KURAL 428

It is folly not to fear what ought to be feared.
So the wise dread what should be dreaded.

KURAL 429

Fearsome sufferings shall never happen
to knowing ones who guard against future happenings.

KURAL 430

Those who possess wisdom possess everything.
Whatever others possess, without wisdom they have nothing.

வருமுன்னர்க் காவாதான் வாழ்க்கை எரிமுன்னர்
வைத்தூறு போலக் கெடும்.

Guarding Against Faults

KURAL 431

Those who are free from vanity, vulgarity and venomousness
will prosper in deserving dignity.

KURAL 432

Avarice, arrogance and crude amusements are flaws
in the character of an unfit king.

KURAL 433

Though their fault be as small as a millet seed,
to those who dread disgrace it will appear as large as a palm tree.

KURAL 434

One's own faults are one's mortal enemies.
It follows that to guard against them is life's gravest concern.

KURAL 435

The good fortune of a man who does not guard against failings
before they manifest will perish like a stack of straw before a fire.

KURAL 436

What fault remains in a king who expunges his own faults
before examining the faults in others?

KURAL 437

The wealth of him who, out of avarice, fails to do what
should be done will vanish without the slightest vestige.

KURAL 438

When all faults are reckoned, one remains unrivaled:
the greedy grasping known as avarice.

KURAL 439

Never indulge in admiring yourself.
Never be drawn toward deeds that do not benefit others.

KURAL 440

Delighting in life's pleasures in guarded privacy
nullifies the conspiring schemes of enemies.

தம்மிற் பெரியார்
தமரா ஒழுகுதல்
வன்மையு ளெல்லாந் தலை.

Gaining Support from the Great

KURAL 441

If men fathom what it means to have virtuous and wise friends,
they will find the means to procure such friendships.

KURAL 442

There are men who allay today's trials and avert
tomorrow's troubles. Befriend and look after them.

KURAL 443

To cherish and befriend men of greatness
is the rarest of all rare things.

KURAL 444

A man's greatest strength is meriting friendship
with those greater than himself.

KURAL 445

Knowing that they function as a monarch's eyes,
a king looks at ministers meticulously before engaging them.

KURAL 446

A man's foes are rendered ineffective
if he can live in fellowship with the worthy.

KURAL 447

Who can destroy the man who enjoys the friendship
of aides who will not hesitate to admonish him?

KURAL 448

With no one to reprove and thus protect him,
a king will be destroyed, though no one seeks his destruction.

KURAL 449

Profit is not for those who have no capital; nor is stability
for those who lack the support of faithful friends.

KURAL 450

While it is perilous to make a multitude of foes,
it is ten times worse to give up the friendship of the worthy.

சிற்றினம் அஞ்சும் பெருமை சிறுமைதான்
சுற்றமாச் சூழ்ந்து விடும்.

Avoidance of Base Company

KURAL 451
Men of greatness dread base company,
while the low-minded consider them kinsmen.

KURAL 452
As water changes according to the soil through which it flows,
so a man assimilates the character of his associates.

KURAL 453
By knowing his thoughts, a man's mind is discovered.
By knowing his associates, his character is revealed.

KURAL 454
Wisdom, appearing to originate in a man's mind,
has its source in his companions.

KURAL 455
Purity of mind and purity of conduct—these two
depend upon the purity of a man's companions.

KURAL 456
Praiseworthy progeny come to pure-minded men
whose pure companions keep impure deeds away.

KURAL 457
Wealth will be bestowed on good-minded men,
and all renown will be granted by good company.

KURAL 458
Even perfect men, possessing the mind's full goodness,
are fortified by pious fellowship.

KURAL 459
Goodness of mind leads to bliss in the next world,
and even that is secured by the company of good men.

KURAL 460
There exists no greater aid than virtuous fellowship,
and no greater affliction than evil fraternity.

எண்ணித் துணிக கரும் துணிந்தபின்
எண்ணுவம் என்பது இழுக்கு.

Deliberate Before Acting

KURAL 461

When action is needed, ponder what is to be gained,
what lost, and what ultimately achieved, then proceed.

KURAL 462

There is nothing too difficult for a man who, before he acts,
deliberates with chosen friends and reflects privately.

KURAL 463

The wise never undertake an enterprise that rashly risks
existing capital to reach for potential profits.

KURAL 464

Those who dread ridicule and disgrace
will not commence any task that is unclear.

KURAL 465

To sally forth without a well-conceived plan
is one way to cultivate an enemy's strength.

KURAL 466

Doing what should not be done will bring ruin,
and not doing what should be done will also bring ruin.

KURAL 467

Embark upon an action after careful thought. It is folly to say,
"Let us begin the task now and think about it later."

KURAL 468

Any task not methodically performed may go awry,
though men in multitudes support it.

KURAL 469

Even in doing good deeds a man may err
if he does not consider the recipient's unique nature.

KURAL 470

Having made his plans, let a man keep his actions above blame.
The world will never approve of acts that are beneath him.

பீலிபெய் சாகாடும் அச்சிறும் அப்பண்டஞ்
சால மிகுத்துப் பெயின்.

Understanding Strength

KURAL 471

The prudent man acts after weighing the strength a deed demands,
his own strength and the strengths of allies and opposition.

KURAL 472

Nothing is impossible for those who perceive the nature and means
of their task and proceed with determination.

KURAL 473

Ignorant of their strengths, many plunge zealously
into projects, only to miscarry midway.

KURAL 474

How swiftly men who praise themselves perish, unappraised of
their real measure, unable to live in peace with others.

KURAL 475

Load too many of them, and even peacock feathers
would break a sturdy cart's axle.

KURAL 476

He who has climbed out to the tip of a tree branch
and attempts to climb farther will forfeit his life.

KURAL 477

Know the measure of your capacity to give, then give accordingly;
such clarity is the way wealth is preserved.

KURAL 478

A small income is no cause for failure,
provided expenditures do not exceed it.

KURAL 479

Prosperous as his life may appear, unless a man
measures well his wealth, it will disappear without a trace.

KURAL 480

How swiftly a generous man's riches dwindle and die,
if he does not evaluate the limits of his means.

கொக்கொக்க கூம்பும் பருவத்து மற்றதன்
குத்தொக்க சீர்த்த இடத்து.

Understanding Timeliness

KURAL 481

During the day, a crow can overcome the more powerful owl.
Desiring to defeat his enemy, a king must pick the proper time.

KURAL 482

A man may tightly bind himself to prosperity
by the tether called timely action.

KURAL 483

Is there any task too difficult for the man who acts
at the right time and with the proper means?

KURAL 484

One may aim to acquire the whole world and succeed,
if actions target the right time and place.

KURAL 485

Those who aim to own the world
must wait, unruffled, for the fitting hour.

KURAL 486

The powerful man's patient restraint is like the drawing back
of the fighting ram before he strikes the stunning blow.

KURAL 487

When irate, clear-minded men never show it then and there.
Holding it within, they watch for an opportune moment.

KURAL 488

Bow ever so humbly when meeting an enemy.
His own head will hang humiliated when, in time, he meets defeat.

KURAL 489

When a rare opportunity comes your way, do not hesitate
to swiftly accomplish otherwise impossible tasks.

KURAL 490

There are times to stay still as a stalking heron.
There are times to move swiftly as a heron strikes.

காலாழ் களிரில் நரியடும் கண்ணஞ்சா
வேலான் முகத்த களிறு.

Understanding the Right Place

KURAL 491

Neither ridicule the opposition nor initiate an offensive
until you possess a strategic place from which to strike.

KURAL 492

In battle, a fortified position yields plentiful advantages,
even to those already possessing power and prowess.

KURAL 493

Even the weak may prevail if they pick the right field of action,
establish good defenses and then fight well.

KURAL 494

When an attacker lays siege from a strategic location,
his enemy's thoughts of conquest become unthinkable.

KURAL 495

In a river's depths the crocodile is unconquerable,
but others may defeat him if he leaves those waters.

KURAL 496

A massive chariot with mighty wheels cannot sail the sea;
nor can an ocean-going ship traverse the land.

KURAL 497

Fearlessness is the only friend one needs,
if he relentlessly ponders from which place to pounce.

KURAL 498

Even a small army, if well–entrenched, can repel
the power of a large army, forcing it to retreat.

KURAL 499

Even if they are without firm forts and inferior in force,
a people defending their own soil are difficult to defeat.

KURAL 500

The fearless elephant may slaughter a multitude of warriors,
yet be slain by a single jackal if his legs sink in muddy marsh.

குடிப்பிறந்து குற்றத்தின்
நீங்கி வடுப்பரியும்
நாணுடையான் கட்டே தெளிவு.

Testing and Trusting Men

KURAL 501

Pick that man who passes a four-fold test:
how he handles virtue, wealth, pleasure and loss of life.

KURAL 502

Place trust in a man of good family, free from faults,
with a modest nature that dreads reproach.

KURAL 503

Even faultless, deeply learned men, when closely examined,
are rarely found to be entirely free from ignorance.

KURAL 504

Weigh a man's merits and weigh his faults,
then judge him according to the greater.

KURAL 505

The touchstone that discloses a man's greatness
or smallness is simply this: his deeds.

KURAL 506

Beware of trusting men who have no kin.
Unattached to people, they are unashamed of misdeeds.

KURAL 507

When a man employs a know-nothing out of affection,
he engages all kinds of foolishness.

KURAL 508

To trust a stranger without investigation invites troubles
so endless that even descendants must endure them.

KURAL 509

Without investigation, trust no one. Having investigated,
entrust a man with matters for which he is trustworthy.

KURAL 510

To trust a man who has not been tested and to suspect a man
who has proven trustworthy lead alike to endless ills.

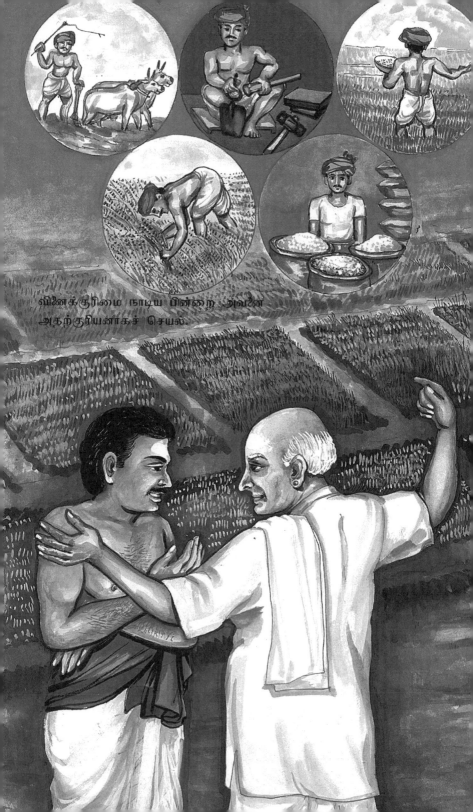

வினைக்குறிமை நாடிய பின்றை அதற்குரியனாகச் செயல்.

Testing and Employing Men

KURAL 511

Employ men who discern the good and the bad
in every situation and naturally choose the good.

KURAL 512

Let him do the work who can increase profits,
spread prosperity and search out problems.

KURAL 513

He alone is trustworthy who fully possesses these four:
kindness, intelligence, assurance and freedom from greed.

KURAL 514

Though tested fully in simulated settings,
many men function differently under working conditions.

KURAL 515

Work should be entrusted to men based on their knowledge
and diligence and not merely on bonds of affection.

KURAL 516

Consider the work, choose the workman,
calculate the timing with care, then commence.

KURAL 517

Having decided, "This man is qualified to do this
work in this way," leave him alone to perform it.

KURAL 518

After ascertaining what work befits a man,
assign him to a fitting function.

KURAL 519

Wealth withdraws from the man who refuses to acknowledge
the informal friendliness his workers wish to share with him.

KURAL 520

The king should scrutinize his staff's conduct daily.
If they do not go astray, the world will not go astray.

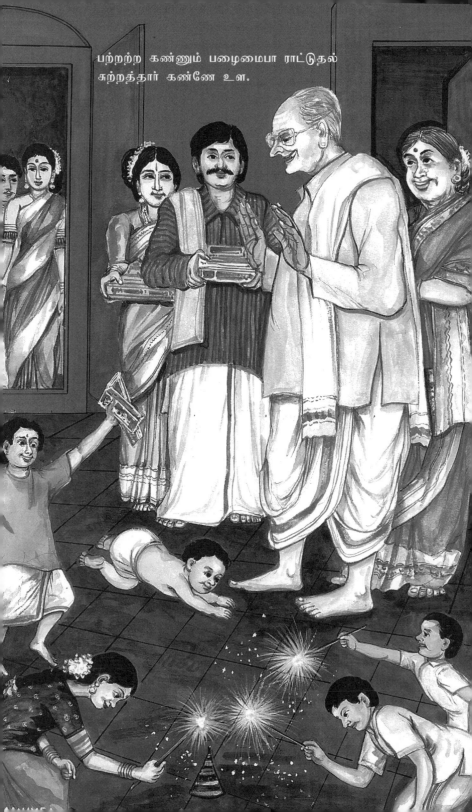

பற்றற்ற கண்ணும் பழைமைபா ராட்டுதல்
சுற்றத்தார் கண்ணே உள.

Fellowship of Kindred

KURAL 521
Should a man's wealth disappear, only his kinsmen
will maintain their customary kindness.

KURAL 522
If a man's kindred cling to him with unfailing love,
his fortunes will never fail to flourish.

KURAL 523
Pursuing a happy life without mixing with one's clan
is like flooding a pond that has flimsy banks.

KURAL 524
The real profit gained by gaining riches
is that one may then live surrounded by relatives.

KURAL 525
Scores of kin will crowd around the kindly man
who gives generously and speaks sweetly.

KURAL 526
In this wide world none enjoys a more faithful family
than he who hands out large gifts and holds back all anger.

KURAL 527
The crow does not conceal his food, but calls his kind to share it;
prosperity will remain with men of such a nature.

KURAL 528
The multitudes thrive when they observe their monarch
observing each one's merits, not seeing mere sameness in all.

KURAL 529
Close kinsmen who have become estranged
will come back when the cause of disagreement goes away.

KURAL 530
When one who left him returns with justifying reason,
the ruler may, after careful reflection, accept him back.

பொச்சாப்பார்க் கில்லே
புகழ்வை அது உலகத்து
எப்பால்நூ லோர்க்கும் துணிவு.

Avoiding Unmindfulness

KURAL 531
Excessive anger's harm is exceeded
by excessive merriment's mindless mishaps.

KURAL 532
Just as perpetual poverty slowly nullifies one's knowledge,
so frequent forgetfulness destroys one's prestige.

KURAL 533
Unmindful men will never know renown.
This is the verdict of every virtuous text in the world.

KURAL 534
Nothing will provide defense for the cowardly,
and nothing will secure good for the unmindful.

KURAL 535
The forgetful man who fails to take precautions
against impending perils will regret his negligence afterwards.

KURAL 536
Nothing can compare to watchfulness
extended unfailingly to all people at all times.

KURAL 537
There is nothing too difficult for the man who
consciously conceives and carefully executes his work.

KURAL 538
One should do that which men extol as praiseworthy.
Forgetfully failing to do so brings deprivation lasting seven births.

KURAL 539
Whenever the mind is engrossed in pleasant infatuations,
one should remember men who were ruined by forgetfulness.

KURAL 540
It is easy to get what you think of
if you can get yourself to think of it.

கொல்லியிற கொடியாரை வேந்தொறுத்தல்
பைங்கூழ்கிளீகட் டதனோடு நேர்.

Just Reign

KURAL 541

Investigate well, show favor to none, maintain impartiality,
consult the law, then give judgment—that is the way of justice.

KURAL 542

All the world looks to the rain cloud for sustenance.
All the people look to the king's scepter for protection.

KURAL 543

Even the *Vedas* of the *brahmins* and all dharma therein
rely on the sovereign's sturdy staff for sustenance.

KURAL 544

The world embraces the feet of a great kingdom's monarch
who lovingly embraces subjects under his justice-wielding scepter.

KURAL 545

Rain and rich harvests arise together
in a country whose sovereign ruler raises his rod lawfully.

KURAL 546

Victory is not won by the lance,
but by the king's scepter, provided it is not crooked.

KURAL 547

The potentate protects the whole world,
and Justice protects him if he does not stray from Her.

KURAL 548

An inaccessible ruler who listens and adjudicates inattentively
will inevitably plummet from power and perish.

KURAL 549

No fault befalls a king who, in guarding and caring for his subjects,
punishes wrongdoers—for that is his duty.

KURAL 550

A ruler's punishing cruel criminals by execution
is like a gardener's removing weeds from his garden.

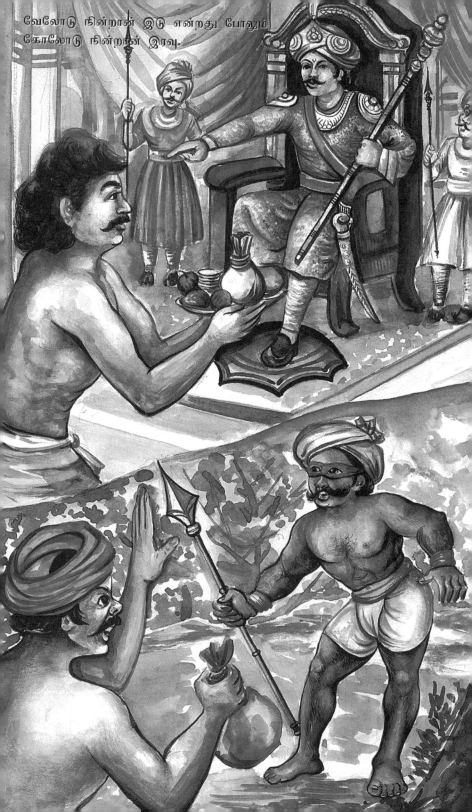

வேலோடு நின்றான் இடு என்றது போலும்
கோலோடு நின்றான் இரவு.

Unjust Reign

KURAL 551

More malicious than a professional murderer is the monarch
who rules his people with injustice and oppression.

KURAL 552

A scepter-wielding king requesting a gift is like
a lance-bearing robber demanding, "Give me all you have."

KURAL 553

Day to day the king must seek out and punish unlawfulness,
or day by day his country will plummet toward ruin.

KURAL 554

Without thinking, a king rules crookedly, and thus
forfeits his subjects' loyalty, together with his own fortune.

KURAL 555

Are not the tears of a people who cannot bear their monarch's
oppressive reign the force that erodes his prosperity?

KURAL 556

Ruling rightly, a monarch may long endure.
Without that, his majesty is rightfully unenduring.

KURAL 557

As the Earth fares under a rainless sky,
so do a people languish under an unkind king.

KURAL 558

Possessions hold less pleasure than poverty
for oppressed subjects living under an unjust king.

KURAL 559

If the king acts contrary to justice, contrary seasons will befall
the land and rain-laden clouds will fail to come forth.

KURAL 560

If the people's protector fails to protect
brahmins will forget the *Vedas* and cows' milk will dry up.

வெருவந்த செய்தொழுகும்
வெங்கோல நாயின்
ஒருவந்தம் ஒல்லைக் கெடும்.

Avoidance of Tyranny

KURAL 561

He is a true king who impartially investigates
and then duly punishes so that the offense will not recur.

KURAL 562

He who wishes his prosperity to long remain
will raise the rod severely, but let it fall softly.

KURAL 563

The tyrant who causes dread in his people
will perish quickly and inevitably.

KURAL 564

"Our king is cruel." When these bitter words are spoken,
the monarch's life is shortened, and he soon succumbs.

KURAL 565

If a man's countenance is harsh and access to him is hard,
his wealth, however vast, might as well belong to a demon.

KURAL 566

If a man is unkind and speaks cruelly,
his vast wealth will not last long before perishing.

KURAL 567

Harsh language and overly severe punishment,
like a keen file, grind down a king's conquering powers.

KURAL 568

A king's wealth wanes when, without thoughtful involvement,
he lets ministers work, then furiously faults their efforts.

KURAL 569

The sovereign who does not secure defenses will be seized
by fear when wartime comes and promptly perish.

KURAL 570

Earth bears no greater burden than crude counselors
that a cruel-sceptered king binds to his court.

கண்ணோட்டம் என்னும் கழிபெருங் காரிகை
உண்மையான் உண்டிவ் உலகு.

The Kindly Look

KURAL 571

The fairest graciousness, they say, is a kindly look.
Wherever it thrives, the whole world flourishes.

KURAL 572

It is compassion that sustains the world's existence.
The existence of those bereft of it is a burden to the Earth.

KURAL 573

What use is melody in an unmusical song?
What use are eyes that express no sympathy?

KURAL 574

Other than being facial ornaments, what do eyes
with no quality of kindness really do?

KURAL 575

A compassionate glance is the eyes' true ornament.
Without such kindness, eyes become unsightly sores.

KURAL 576

Eyes that remain unmoved by pity might as well
be unmovable tree stumps bound in earth.

KURAL 577

Those who lack a kindly look are indeed without eyes,
and those who truly have eyes never lack a gracious look.

KURAL 578

This world belongs to those who, while neglecting no duty,
never neglect to behold others benevolently.

KURAL 579

To grant forbearing kindness even to those
who aggrieve us is the foremost of virtues.

KURAL 580

Desiring to be gracious above all else, guests may politely accept
even poison they watched their host prepare and serve.

ஒற்றும் உரைசான்ற
நூலும் இவையிரண்டும்
தெற்றென்க மன்னவன் கண்.

Espionage

KURAL 581

Competent spies and the respected codes of law—
consider these two the eyes of a king.

KURAL 582

Duty requires the monarch to swiftly acquire
knowledge of all happenings among all men each day.

KURAL 583

Without assessing the intelligence reports of informants,
a king can never achieve victory.

KURAL 584

The working staff, close kindred and known enemies—
all such people are the legitimate study of spies.

KURAL 585

An able spy is one who can assume an unsuspicious disguise,
is fearless when caught and never betrays his secrets.

KURAL 586

Disguised as a monk or a mendicant, the master spy
moves about investigating all, never careless, come what may.

KURAL 587

A spy must ferret out hidden facts,
assuring himself that knowledge found is beyond doubt.

KURAL 588

Before believing one spy's espionage,
have another spy espy the information.

KURAL 589

See that informants do not know one another,
and accept their findings only when three reports agree.

KURAL 590

One must not openly honor operatives.
To do so is to divulge one's deepest secrets.

வெள்ளத் தூனய மலர்நீட்டம் மாந்தர்தம்
உள்ளத் தூனயது உயர்வு.

Possession of Industriousness

KURAL 591

Possessing belongs only to the industrious. Do those
who lack such energy really possess their possessions?

KURAL 592

Those who own a mental energy possess a thing of worth.
Material wealth is an unenduring possession that goes away.

KURAL 593

Those who possess persevering industry
will never say in despair, "We have lost our wealth."

KURAL 594

Good fortune of its own accord ferrets out and
finds the man of unflagging energy.

KURAL 595

The length of the lotus stalk depends on the water's depth.
Even so, a man's greatness is proportionate to his mind's energy.

KURAL 596

Let all thoughts be thoughts of noble progress,
for then even failing cannot be called a failure.

KURAL 597

Elephants stand firm even when wounded by a barrage of arrows.
Strong-willed men are not discouraged when they meet disaster.

KURAL 598

Without a zealous spirit, one will never enjoy
the proud exhilaration of the world's generosity.

KURAL 599

The towering elephant, with his tapering tusks,
still shrinks in fear when a fierce tiger attacks.

KURAL 600

An industrious mind is a man's real wealth.
Lacking it, he is immobile—more tree-like than human.

இடிபுரிந்து எள்ளுஞ்சொல் கேட்பர் மடிபுரிந்து
மாண்ட உளுற்றி லவர்.

Avoidance of Idleness

KURAL 601
The eternal flame of a family vanishes
when eclipsed by that dark cloud called idleness.

KURAL 602
Let those who wish their family to be a noble family
call laziness "laziness" and live without it.

KURAL 603
The simpleton whose actions are stifled by ruinous indolence
will see his family perish before he dies.

KURAL 604
Their families decrease and their vices increase when men,
ensnared in sloth, do not put forth earnest effort.

KURAL 605
Procrastination, forgetfulness, sloth and sleep—
these four shape the ship bearing those destined for ruin.

KURAL 606
Seldom do languid men achieve anything special,
even when supported by the world's wealthy proprietors.

KURAL 607
Idle men, incapable of honorable exertion,
invite scorn and suffer the shame of scolding words.

KURAL 608
If languor is allowed to linger in aristocrats,
they will be forced into servitude under foes.

KURAL 609
Disgrace that has come upon a man and his family
will disappear the moment he casts out laziness.

KURAL 610
A king devoid of indolence will thereby procure all that
cosmic expanse measured by God's immeasurable strides.

மடியுளான் மாமுகடி
என்ப மடியிலான்
தாளுளாள் தாமரையி னாள்.

Perseverance

KURAL 611

Never say in weakness, "This task is too difficult."
Perseverance will confer the ability to accomplish it.

KURAL 612

Beware of leaving any work undone, remembering that the world
abandons those who abandon their work unfinished.

KURAL 613

The pride of profuse giving dwells only
with the dignity of diligent effort.

KURAL 614

Like the swordsmanship of an effeminate man, the philanthropy
of those who avoid hard work will end in failure.

KURAL 615

Standing like a pillar, he who prefers work to pleasure
supports his family and sweeps away their every sad sorrow.

KURAL 616

Perseverance generates prosperity,
and the lack of it engenders poverty.

KURAL 617

They say the black ogress called Misfortune lurks in laziness,
while Goddess Fortune lingers in the laboring toils of active men.

KURAL 618

To be destitute of good fortune is no one's disgrace, but shame
belongs to those devoid of wisdom and tenacity.

KURAL 619

Though destiny decrees that one's deeds will fail,
the wages for determined work are always paid.

KURAL 620

Those who strive with tireless exertion and remain undaunted
will live to behold the backside of retreating Fate.

மடுத்தாவா யெல்லாம் பகடன்னான் உற்ற
இடுக்கண் இடர்ப்பாடு உடைத்து.

Being Undaunted by Troubles

KURAL 621

Laugh when troubles come your way.
Nothing conquers calamity better than that.

KURAL 622

A tide of troubles will recede the moment
an intelligent man's mind collects itself to face them.

KURAL 623

Trouble itself they send away troubled
who do not trouble themselves at the sight of it.

KURAL 624

Troubles will feel troubled facing a man who faces them
like the determined bullock that wades through every difficulty.

KURAL 625

Though massed upon him like a mountain,
a man's afflictions will be crushed by his undaunted will.

KURAL 626

Those who do not clutch their wealth, boasting, "I have so much,"
will not, in poorer times, bemoan, "I have so little."

KURAL 627

Knowing this body to be the prey of misery,
high souls, expecting troubles, do not find them troublesome.

KURAL 628

Declaring difficulties to be perfectly natural,
those who do not pursue life's pleasures will not suffer its sorrows.

KURAL 629

He who does not long for joy in joy
will not suffer sorrow in sorrow.

KURAL 630

The man who does not distinguish pain from pleasure
becomes so distinguished that even enemies hope to pay homage.

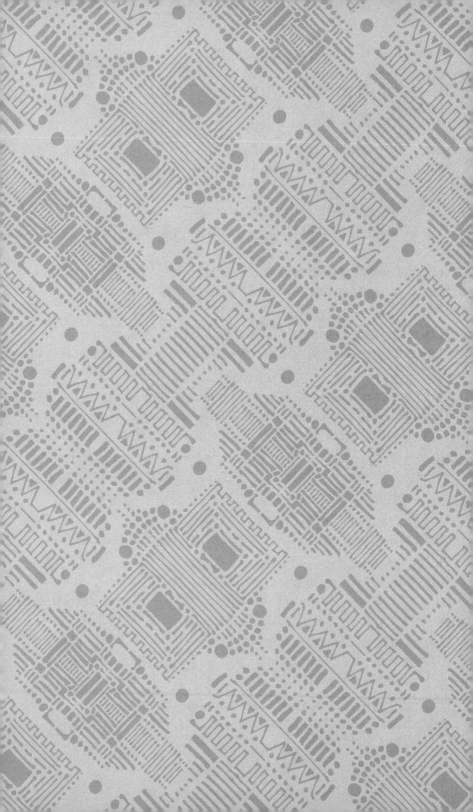

Amaicchiyal
அமைச்சியல்

கடனறிந்து காலம் கருதி இடனறிந்து
எண்ணி யுரைப்பான் தலை.

Section VI
Ministers

KURAL 687
He is unsurpassed who knows duty and place,
judges the suitable time and thinks before he speaks.

HERE WE HAVE A MANUAL THAT IS INVALUABLE FOR THOSE WHO WISH TO TRAIN THEMSELVES TO BECOME USEFUL TO A PRESIDENT, PRIME MINISTER, king or any head of state, CEO of a corporation or to become a Senator, Congressman or military leader—all jobs that are today more complex and sophisticated than any prime minister's in the courts of the weaver's day. These verses are explicit, helpful and informative, even to managers and workers who aspire to be first-rate second men. It is amazing that Valluvar has been able to accomplish offering so much of practical advice in so few words. Any corporate manual would have used hundreds of pages to explain what he illumines in ten— a total of one hundred verses explaining everything from what a minister must do to attain and maintain his office to the necessity of having no dread of speaking to an audience.

It is here that we can see into the politics of two thousand years ago and sense the society that existed in the centuries before Valluvar lived and, reaching its height, led to his making these observations so eloquently and pricelessly. This one section of the book has been memorized and taken to heart, put into practice, by councilmen, barristers and political personages as well as religious leaders and others whose mission it is to articulate their cause. Chapters 64 through 73 belong to everyone who has a calling. Actors, journeymen, salespeople, graduates and soon-to-be graduates of any field will find the verses in section six of *Weaver's Wisdom* most helpful.

It was the literary style in those far-off days to write concisely. The weaver chose a difficult form, usually four words in the first line and three in the second line—seven measures in all. This concise, disciplined style is easily memorized, placed into the subconscious mind to later manifest in action, for a change in beliefs makes a change in attitude, and this in turn changes the image of the person, to himself as well as to others. Finally, all that the verses so memorized contain become his personality, his mode of operation and who he is.

We can do the same, now that the same verses are available in modern English. Choose those you want to mold yourself into. Memorize them, read and reread them nightly just before sleep. When you are most sleepy is the best time for their meaning to slip into the subconscious mind. Then, during the night, the mind of the soul, the superconscious, will work with the subconscious, and slowly, ever so slowly, a transformation into the new you will occur.

In the chapter on associating with monarchs are invaluable bits of advice. Then we have the advice of intuiting another's thoughts by reading facial expressions, body movements and all that is unspoken—a valued tool for any leader or one aspiring to a higher position in any occupation. For the public speaker, the weaver gives a lesson in judging an audience, describing all the good that will happen as well as all the problems to be expected by failure to heed this advice. Discussing how to deal with opposition as well as success, he advises, "Before acting, resolve all doubts by pondering five points: cost, means, time, place and the action itself." Many a failed business, small or large, would still be in business today had the owners but known and followed these five points.

In chapter 66 Valluvar explains the difference between good money earned by right means and bad money earned by wrongful means. This advice involves the never-flinching law of karma. Wrongful acquisition, such as accepting bribes or, worse, give them, slowly destroys the morality of the community. Money earned from illegal enterprises has bad karmic consequences: You can't do good things with bad money. It can never, ever be cleansed.

Ministers

KURAL 631

A minister is he who can conceive a great enterprise,
rightly choose the ways, means and time, then carry it out.

KURAL 632

Added to the above five, a minister is well-endowed with
steadfastness, learning, perseverance and protection of the people.

KURAL 633

He who can divide ememies, bind friends more firmly
and reunite estranged allies is unequivocally a minister.

KURAL 634

Call him a minister who comprehends things,
effectively executes them and competently directs others.

KURAL 635

The helpful aide understands codes of conduct, discerns what is
fitting in every situation and speaks with learned deliberation.

KURAL 636

When shrewd intelligence combines with scholastic study,
who can stand before such peerless subtlety?

KURAL 637

Though thoroughly learned in theoretical methods,
one should act only after fathoming the world's proven practices.

KURAL 638

The loyal minister's duty is to communicate his counsel,
even if his leader is a dullard who spurns advice.

KURAL 639

Better for the king to face 700 million far-off foes
than to retain a single counselor who conspires at his side.

KURAL 640

Little matter that they can devise the perfect plan;
those without executive skills never finish their work.

விரைந்து தொழில்கேட்கும் ஞாலம் நிரந்தினிது
சொல்லுதல் வல்லார்ப் பெறின்.

Eloquence

KURAL 641
Among a man's many good possessions,
none can equal having a good tongue.

KURAL 642
Prosperity and ruin issue from the power of the tongue.
Therefore, guard yourself against thoughtless speech.

KURAL 643
The substance of artful speech holds friends spell-bound,
and its eloquence enchants even enemies.

KURAL 644
Judge the nature of your listeners and speak accordingly.
There is nothing more virtuous or valuable than this.

KURAL 645
Speak out your speech after ascertaining that
no speech can be spoken to refute that speech.

KURAL 646
To speak so that listeners long to hear more and to listen so that
others' meaning is grasped are ideals of the impeccably great.

KURAL 647
In a war of words, none can defeat a persuasive man
who never succumbs to fear or forgetfulness.

KURAL 648
Upon finding men whose forceful speech is couched
in cogent and enchanting ways, the world swiftly gathers around.

KURAL 649
Unaware of the artful use of a few flawless words,
men become enamored with excessive verbiage.

KURAL 650
Men who cannot communicate their knowledge to others
resemble a bouquet of unfragrant flowers in full bloom.

அழக்கொண்ட எல்லாம்
அழப்போம் இழப்பினும்
பிற்பயக்கும் நற்பா லவை.

Purity of Action

KURAL 651

Good friendships bring wealth to a man,
but goodness of action fulfills his every wish.

KURAL 652

Fame-garnering actions of no real benefit
should always be strictly avoided.

KURAL 653

Declaring that their future will be brighter,
men must desist from deeds that darken glory's light.

KURAL 654

However troubled the times, men of imperturbable perception
never commit shameful or sordid deeds.

KURAL 655

Do nothing that would make you regret, "What have I done!"
However, if regrettable deeds occur, do not remain regretful.

KURAL 656

Though he must behold his own mother's hunger,
let a man desist from deeds condemned by wise men.

KURAL 657

The worst poverty of worthy men is more worthwhile
than the greatest wealth amassed by wrongful means.

KURAL 658

Forbidden deeds, however well accomplished, inflict sorrow
on those who seek after rather than shun them.

KURAL 659

What is gained by tears will go by tears. Even if it begins
with loss, in the end, goodness gives many good things.

KURAL 660

Protecting the country with wrongly garnered wealth
is like preserving water in an unbaked clay pot.

உருவுகண்டு எள்ளாமை வேண்டும்
உருள்பெருந்தேர்க்கு
அச்சாணி அன்னார் உடைத்து.

Resoluteness of Action

KURAL 661

What is called resoluteness of action is, in truth,
resoluteness of mind. It is a quality unlike any other.

KURAL 662

Avoiding all failure-prone action and remaining undiscouraged by
failures are said to be the dual directives of wise men.

KURAL 663

Revealing an action after its completion is resoluteness.
Disclosing an action midway causes endless misery.

KURAL 664

It is easy for anyone to speak of a plan,
but difficult indeed to execute what has been spoken.

KURAL 665

Strong-willed exploits of virtuous men
win the crown's respect and the crowd's acclaim.

KURAL 666

Those who think will have their thoughts fulfilled,
just as they thought, provided they possess strength of will.

KURAL 667

Do not disparage men who appear small, for there are those,
seemingly insignificant, who are like the linchpin of a mighty chariot.

KURAL 668

Visualize actions with unclouded clarity,
then forcefully undertake them without delay or indecision.

KURAL 669

Despite dire hardships, hold to strength of mind
and do those deeds which yield joy of heart.

KURAL 670

The world has no use for those who have no use for resolute
action, whatever other strengths they may possess.

வினையான் வினையாக்கிக்
கோடல் நுணகவுள்
யானையால் யானையாத்
தற்று

Modes of Action

KURAL 671
Deliberation ends when a decision is reached.
To delay that decision's execution is detrimental.

KURAL 672
Slumber when sleepy work awaits,
but never rest when actions demand sleepless vigilance.

KURAL 673
Direct action is good whenever possible,
but when it is not, seek other means of success.

KURAL 674
Reflect on this: efforts and enemies, if left unfinished,
can both ravage you like an unextinguished fire.

KURAL 675
Before acting, resolve all doubts by pondering five points:
cost, means, time, place and the action itself.

KURAL 676
Discern the outcome of an enterprise, the obstacles and the
opulent earnings that successful effort assures—then act.

KURAL 677
The way to accomplish any task is to ascertain
the inmost thoughts of an expert in that task.

KURAL 678
Just as one elephant may be used to tether another,
so one task may be the means of accomplishing another.

KURAL 679
Before bestowing kind favors on friends,
hasten to befriend those still estranged.

KURAL 680
Sensing with trepidation their peoples' fears, leaders of
minor realms bow and accept the terms of mightier rulers.

தூய்மை துணைமை துணிவுடைமை இம்மூன்றின்
வாய்மை வழியுரைப்பான் பண்பு.

Ambassadors

KURAL 681

Kindliness, high birth and a nature congenial to kings
comprise the innate disposition of an ambassador.

KURAL 682

Kindliness, knowingness and deliberateness of speech
are three necessities a diplomat finds indispensable.

KURAL 683

An envoy sent to announce to lance-bearing monarchs
his own king's imminent victory must be a pandit among pandits.

KURAL 684

Send him on mission who possesses three attractive traits:
well-winnowed wisdom, modest dignity and ample learning.

KURAL 685

Whatever good an ambassador procures derives from succinct
speech, cheerful conversation and avoidance of argument.

KURAL 686

An envoy is educated, eloquently persuasive, unafraid of
the fiercest stare and knows what befits the moment.

KURAL 687

He is unsurpassed who knows duty and place,
judges the suitable time and thinks before he speaks.

KURAL 688

Integrity, influence and intrepidity—these three and truthfulness
are qualities of one who faithfully delivers his monarch's message.

KURAL 689

Commission him to deliver the monarch's mandates
who has a steady gaze and never blurts out flawed words.

KURAL 690

An ambassador fearlessly extends his king's glory,
though he might thereby expend his own life.

அகலாது அணுகாது தீக்காய்வார் போல்க
இகல்வேந்தர்ச் சேர்ந்தொழுகு வார்.

Associating with Monarchs

KURAL 691

Associates of contentious kings should be like men warming
themselves by a fire, moving neither too near nor too far away.

KURAL 692

Do not desire to get what the king desires to have,
and the king himself will confer enduring wealth.

KURAL 693

One wishing to be wary must beware of his own indiscretions.
Once suspicions are aroused, they are rarely removed.

KURAL 694

In the presence of the great ones, never speak
in whispers or exchange smiles with others.

KURAL 695

The emissary neither eavesdrops nor meddles into matters.
Instead, he listens raptly when secrets are revealed.

KURAL 696

Sensing unspoken thoughts and ascertaining the ripe moment,
speak of vital matters amiably, without offending others.

KURAL 697

Speak useful ideas that interest the sovereign.
Always leave useless thoughts unspoken—even if he inquires.

KURAL 698

Never criticize the king because he is young or your own kin.
Rather respect the resplendent dignity that kingship commands.

KURAL 699

Men whose wisdom is unwavering
do not use their high reputation to excuse lowly behavior.

KURAL 700

Men who do unworthy deeds, expecting the king's indulgence
because of a long-standing friendship, warrant their own ruin.

அடுத்தது காட்டும்
பளிங்குபோல் நெஞ்சம்
கடுத்தது காட்டும்
முகம்.

Discerning Unspoken Thoughts

KURAL 701

He who can discern another's unspoken thoughts by merely looking
is an emerald on an Earth encircled by equable seas.

KURAL 702

Regard as god-like those who can divine
without hesitation what is in the minds of others.

KURAL 703

Give whatever is required to gain an advisor
who, knowing his own mind, can read another's intentions.

KURAL 704

Those who grasp others' unspoken thoughts have the same
physical features as most folks—yet how different they are.

KURAL 705

Of what benefit are eyes in a body, if they cannot
by their observing powers perceive another's intentions?

KURAL 706

As a crystal mirror reflects objects that are nearby,
so the face reflects what is foremost in the heart.

KURAL 707

What is more forthrightly profound than the face?
For whether the heart is angry or glad, the face expresses it first.

KURAL 708

If you find a man who understands matters by looking into
the mind, it suffices to stand silently looking into his face.

KURAL 709

If you find men who know the eye's language
the eyes will speak to them of hidden hate and love.

KURAL 710

Observe those who are said to see subtly with their mind's eye—
their singular measuring rod is their eyes.

உணர்வ துடையார்முன் சொல்லல் வளர்வதன்
பாத்தியுள் நீர்சொரிந் தற்று.

Judging the Audience

KURAL 711

Pure men of studied eloquence should study
an audience before speaking deliberate words.

KURAL 712

Let good men who know the orator's art knowingly await
the right moment to articulate their good knowledge.

KURAL 713

Failing to assess an audience before venturing to speak
is to be unaware of the way of words and remain ineffective.

KURAL 714

Be brilliant before brilliant men; but assume
the dullness of pale mortar before dullards.

KURAL 715

Of all good things, the best is the polite reserve
that refrains from speaking first when with elders and superiors.

KURAL 716

To blunder before perceptive, erudite men
is like slipping and falling from a very high place.

KURAL 717

A learned man's learning shines the brightest
among luminaries capable of critiquing his language.

KURAL 718

Speaking to an audience of thinking men
is like watering a bed of growing plants.

KURAL 719

Those who speak good things to good and learned gatherings
should never repeat them to ignorant groups, even forgetfully.

KURAL 720

Expounding to a throng of unfit men
is like pouring sweet nectar into an open gutter.

பகையகத்துச் சாவார் எளியர் அரியர்
அவையகத்து அஞ்சா தவர்.

Not Dreading the Audience

KURAL 721
Unsullied men, skilled in discourse, may speak unfalteringly
before the powerful, provided they understand their audience.

KURAL 722
Only the learned among learned can convincingly express
what they have learned before a learned assembly.

KURAL 723
Men who can brave death on the battlefield are common;
but rare are they who can face an audience without fear.

KURAL 724
Speak confidently before the learned what you have mastered;
and learn from those more learned what you do not know.

KURAL 725
Study the science of logic in order that
you may fearlessly reply in any assembly.

KURAL 726
What can a coward do with a sword?
What can a man who fears an astute council do with books?

KURAL 727
The learning of those who fearfully face an audience
is like the shining saber of effeminate men facing foes.

KURAL 728
Having learned many things, men remain useless
if they cannot speak well in good assemblies.

KURAL 729
Literary men intimidated by gatherings of good men
are said to be inferior to the illiterate.

KURAL 730
Men whose fear of assemblies forbids them to share
their knowledge, though living, may as well be dead.

Araniyal, Kuuliyal, Pataiyiyal
அரணியல், கூழியல், படையியல்

பிணியின்மை செல்வம் விளைவின்பம் ஏமம்
அணியென்ப நாட்டிற்கிவ் வைந்து.

Section VII
Qualities of a Country

KURAL 738

Five ornaments adorn a country: good health, abundant
harvests, wealth, happiness and safety from invasions.

EVERY SEATED PARLIAMENTARIAN, PRESIDENT AND HIS STAFF CAN READILY RELATE TO THE FIRST CHAPTER OF THIS SECTION, DESCRIBING THE MERITS OF A country in stanzas such as these: "Where unfailing fertile fields, worthy men and wealthy merchants come together—that is a country." "Rain waters, underground waters and rivers shed from well-situated mountains, plus strong fortresses, are features of a fine country." "Five ornaments adorn a country: good health, abundant harvests, wealth, happiness and safety from invasions." The wise old weaver urges good relations between politicians and those they serve, saying, "Even if a country acquires all these blessings, it is worth nothing if it lacks harmony between the ruler and the ruled."

We all can strongly relate to the above, now in the twenty-first century, having seen countries come and go, or endure and thrive. Conflict between leaders and their countrymen usually was at the core of those that failed. After explaining about fortresses and the way to attain wealth and protect it, the weaver speaks on the merits of military force, just as important in his day as in ours. In the long, long ago battles were fought over a bargaining table, with lofty bands of well-armed men standing at attention behind each monarch. If it looked as if a bloody battle would cause one side to win and the other to lose, then and there a deal was made. With a standoff occurring between two well-armed citizens on each side, both leaders exchanged gifts, had tea and departed back to their realms peacefully. But nearly always a stronger country overtook a weaker one that could not manage its affairs properly. This was considered to be a duty.

Then the weaver explains what makes up and holds together a country and its government, a family and its elders, a state, county or any group—the essentials of friendship. He says friendship must be cultivated and continue to be cultivated, and false friends, those who are with you when life is good, but when calamity or a problem comes up, are nowhere to be seen or heard from, must be guarded against. They distance themselves to protect whatever they think they have, rather than come forward in the time of need. Good advice, I would say, then as today, for everyone wishing to move forward, is the weaver's wisdom on the testing of friendships. Many suffer today who have joined gangs and found themselves in deep trouble by listening to and being guided by harmful friendships. They should read chapter 82 over and over so when the cycle of exploring new acquaintances comes around again they make the right choices.

The weaver speaks of hatred in a way that would be a credit to any modern psychologist, and he advises how to handle troubled feelings within oneself and among others. Such valuable insights are rarely spoken about today, unless, of course, in technical manuals of the well-informed, such as professional analysts. There is much more of the issues of his time of which he speaks that applies to our time. It is heartening to note that this advice has sustained a nation and a culture in now South India for well over 2,200 years. Tamil Nadu, the land of the Tamil-speaking Dravidian people, an ancient Caucasian branch, is now and has always been their homeland. Now a state of India with a population of sixty million, but formerly an independent empire, it survived, sustained itself and thrived on these 108 chapters of its *Tirukural* throughout the ups and downs, century after century after century.

To this day, the Tamil people are still reading and memorizing this treatise, which is sworn on in their courts of law and permanently enshrined in Chennai's Valluvar Kottam, where every verse is carved in granite in a great hall for all to read, appreciate, learn from and endeavor to live up to.

இருபுனலும் வாய்ந்த மலையும் வருபுனலும்
வல்லரணும் நாட்டிற்கு உறுப்பு.

The Country

KURAL 731
Where unfailingly fertile fields, worthy men
and wealthy merchants come together—that is a country!

KURAL 732
A land coveted for its vast wealth, free from calamities
and yielding in abundance is indeed a country.

KURAL 733
Call that a nation which bears every burden that befalls it,
yet pays in full all tariffs owed to the king.

KURAL 734
Free of famine, endless epidemics and ravaging foes—
now that is a flourishing country.

KURAL 735
Proliferating factions, ruinous subversives and murderous gangs
harassing the king—a real country is free from all these.

KURAL 736
An incomparable state is one never devastated;
yet if devastated, it would not diminish, but prosper.

KURAL 737
Rain waters, underground waters and rivers shed from well-situated
mountains, plus strong fortresses, are features of a fine country.

KURAL 738
Five ornaments adorn a country: good health, abundant harvests,
wealth, happiness and safety from invasions.

KURAL 739
A land where prosperity comes easily deserves the name *country*,
not one where wealth entails laborious toil.

KURAL 740
Even if a country acquires all these blessings, it is worth nothing
if it lacks harmony between the ruler and the ruled.

மணிநீரும் மண்ணும் மலையும் அணிநிழற்
காடும் உடையது அரண்.

Fortresses

KURAL 741
A fortress is a strategic asset both to aggressors
and to those in fear who seek defense.

KURAL 742
An effective fort has crystal-clear water, arable lands,
a hill and lovely shaded woods.

KURAL 743
The expert texts ordain four features for a fort's barricades:
that they be high, thick, solid and impregnable.

KURAL 744
The ideal fortress is spacious, vulnerable in very few places
and, of itself, defies a determined foe's designs to storm it.

KURAL 745
A good garrison is hard to assail, amply provisioned
and accommodates inmates well.

KURAL 746
The most formidable fortress, stocked with all needed goods,
still needs men of good stock to fend off attack.

KURAL 747
Whether by hurling artillery, tunneling beneath or encircling
to lay siege, it is impossible to capture a strong fort.

KURAL 748
However forcefully assailants may press,
a secure fortress promises allies defense and foes defeat.

KURAL 749
A fortress earns greatness by enabling courageous defenders
to gloriously defeat the enemy at the battle's very onset.

KURAL 750
Whatever excellent qualities a fortress may possess,
it will be of no avail without men of excellent action.

குன்றேறி யானைப்போர் கண்டற்றால் தன்கைத்தொன்று
உண்டாகச் செய்வான் வீணை.

The Ways of Acquiring Wealth

KURAL 751

There is nothing like wealth for lending consequence
to an inconsequential man.

KURAL 752

Those who have nothing have everyone's contempt,
while the rich are exalted by one and all.

KURAL 753

Wealth is an unfailing lamp whose light
reaches every imaginable land, dispelling darkness.

KURAL 754

Riches acquired by mindful means, in a manner
that harms no one, will bring both piety and pleasure.

KURAL 755

Wealth acquired without compassion and love
is to be cast off, not embraced.

KURAL 756

Wealth with no owner, wealth of defeated foes, wealth from
tax and customs—these constitute the royal revenues.

KURAL 757

Compassion, which is the child of Love,
requires for its care the bountiful nurse called Wealth.

KURAL 758

Undertaking an enterprise with sufficient resources in hand
is like standing on a hilltop watching elephants fight below.

KURAL 759

Make money—that is the sharpest scalpel
for paring down an enemy's pride.

KURAL 760

Having acquired affluence, the acquisition of two
other treasures—duty and delight—is effortless.

ஒலித்தக்கால் என்னாம் உவரி எலிப்பகை
நாகம் உயிர்ப்பக் கெடும்.

Merits of the Army

KURAL 761

Foremost among a monarch's possessions stands
a conquering army, complete and fearless.

KURAL 762

Only seasoned soldiers remain bravely determined
when onslaughts decimate them and threaten defeat.

KURAL 763

So what if a legion of rats roars like the raging sea?
The mere hiss of a cobra will deaden their din.

KURAL 764

Commanding a long tradition of valor, acquainted
with neither defeat nor desertion—that defines an army.

KURAL 765

That indeed is an army which stands together,
even when faced with death's grim fury.

KURAL 766

Valor, honor, trustworthiness and a tradition nobly upheld—
these four are an army's protective armor.

KURAL 767

Well-trained armed forces will withstand every attack,
then outflank and storm the foe.

KURAL 768

Even without a winning offense and defense,
an army of splendid appearance may still win acclaim.

KURAL 769

An army will prevail as long as there is
no desertion, no privation and no contention.

KURAL 770

Though courageous troops abound,
there can be no army without commanders.

கைவேல் களிற்றொடு போக்கி வருபவன்
மெய்வேல் பறியா நகும்.

Military Pride

KURAL 771

Dare you not, my enemies, to stand against my monarch!
Many who did now stand as stone monuments.

KURAL 772

It is more gratifying to carry a lance that missed an elephant
than to hold an arrow that hit a thicket-dwelling rabbit.

KURAL 773

Intrepid courage is what they call valor,
and clemency toward the defeated is its sharp edge.

KURAL 774

Having hurled his spear at a battlefield elephant,
the hero found another piercing his side and grasped it with glee.

KURAL 775

Is it not a disgraceful defeat to the courageous warrior
if his defiant eyes so much as blink when a lance is hurled at him?

KURAL 776

When recounting his days, the heroic soldier regards all those
on which no battle scars were sustained as squandered.

KURAL 777

To fasten the warrior's anklet on one who desires glory
more than life is to decorate heroism with distinction.

KURAL 778

Men of courage who do not fear for their lives in battle do not
forfeit soldierly ardor, even if the king prohibits their fighting.

KURAL 779

Who would dare deride as defeated
men who die fulfilling valor's vow?

KURAL 780

Heroic death that fills the sovereign's eyes with tears
worth begging for and then dying for.

உடுக்கை இழந்தவன் கைபோல ஆங்கே
இடுக்கண் களைவதாம் நட்பு.

Friendship

KURAL 781
What is as difficult to secure as friendship?
And what greater security is there against foes?

KURAL 782
With wise men, friendship waxes like the crescent moon;
with fools, it wanes as surely as the full moon must.

KURAL 783
The bonds that good men share are like good bound books,
revealing new enchantments at each new encounter.

KURAL 784
What matters in making friends is not merrymaking,
but a stern rebuking when friends go astray.

KURAL 785
It is not constant meeting and companionship,
but shared sensibilities that confer the alliance of friendship.

KURAL 786
A smiling face is no sure sign of friendship.
Friendship is found deep within a smiling heart.

KURAL 787
To divert a man from wrong, direct him toward right
and share his sorrow in misfortune is comradeship.

KURAL 788
As swiftly as the hand moves to seize a slipping garment,
friendship acts to assuage a friend's distress.

KURAL 789
Where does Friendship hold her court? It is where friends
find constant support in every possible circumstance.

KURAL 790
To boast, "He means so much to me, and I to him,"
merely belittles a friendship.

குணமும் குடிமையும் குற்றமும் குன்றா
இனனும் அறிந்தியாக்க நட்பு.

Testing Fitness for Friendship

KURAL 791
Nothing is more grievous than friendship formed without first testing, for once adopted, it cannot be abandoned by the faithful.

KURAL 792
Unless it begins with testing and proving,
friendship may end in mortal sorrow.

KURAL 793
Before you befriend him, consider a man's character,
family background, faults and faithful allies.

KURAL 794
Pay any price to possess the friendship
of well-born men who cannot bear rebuke and shame.

KURAL 795
Seek out and befriend those who, speaking out, move you to repent,
reprove your wrongdoing and teach you the right ways.

KURAL 796
There is a benefit even in misfortune, for it is the rod
with which a man may measure the loyalty of friends.

KURAL 797
To give up friendship with fools and quit their company—
such loss is said to be a man's greatest gain.

KURAL 798
Don't dwell on thoughts that dim your spirit.
Don't befriend those who flee you in affliction.

KURAL 799
Even in the hour of death, the thoughts of friends
who left you in your hour of need will hurt the heart.

KURAL 800
Hold tight to friendship with pure men;
let go of unfit fellows, even by paying them off.

நட்பிற் குறுப்புக் கெழுதகைமை மற்றதற்கு
உப்பாதல் சான்றோர் கடன்.

Old Familiarity

KURAL 801
What is old familiarity? It is when neither friend
objects to liberties taken by the other.

KURAL 802
Liberties taken by a friend are friendship's rightful possession;
to allow them is the willing duty of wise men.

KURAL 803
What is the purpose of long-standing fellowship
if friends' familiar actions are not accepted as one's own?

KURAL 804
Familiar with familiarity, the wise are never annoyed
when friends do things without asking.

KURAL 805
When friends do things that hurt you, attribute it
to unawareness or to the privileges of friendship.

KURAL 806
Bound by brotherhood, true friends never break their bond
with an old comrade, even if he brings them loss.

KURAL 807
Old friends do not forsake loving fellowships,
even when those they cherish happen to do them harm.

KURAL 808
An intimate of any strength will never listen to faults said of friends;
and on the day a friend offends, he is content to keep silent.

KURAL 809
The world cherishes faithful men who never forsake
old friendships, worn by time but unbroken.

KURAL 810
Even ill-wishers will wish those well
who never abandon affection for old friends.

அமராகத்து ஆற்றறுக்கும் கல்லாமா அன்னார்
தமரின் தனிமை தூல.

Harmful Friendship

KURAL 811

Though unscrupulous men may seem to consume you in friendship,
their companionship grows more delightful as it declines.

KURAL 812

What does it matter if one gains or loses the friendship
of manipulators who befriend to gain and otherwise forsake?

KURAL 813

Prostitutes, thieves and people who make friends
to make money are all alike.

KURAL 814

Some men are like an untrained horse that throws its rider
on the battlefield. Loneliness is better than their friendship.

KURAL 815

Better to give up than to gain the friendship of inferior men
who stay away when they should stay and help.

KURAL 816

The enmity of the wise is ten million times
better than intimate friendship with fools.

KURAL 817

An enemy's rancor is a hundred million times more worthwhile
than companionship with fellows who always clown around.

KURAL 818

If friends feign inability to discharge reasonable tasks,
remain silent and gradually give up their friendship.

KURAL 819

The fellowship of men whose acts
belie their spoken words is bitter, even in dreams.

KURAL 820

There are men who will cherish you in private but censure you
in public—avoid their every befriending approach.

தொழுதகை யுள்ளும்
படையொடுங்கும் ஒன்னார்
அழுதகண் ணீரும் அனைத்து.

False Friendship

KURAL 821
The friendship of those who feign affection is an anvil
on which they hammer you when the opportunity arises.

KURAL 822
For those who act like friends, but are not,
friendship fluctuates like a fickle woman.

KURAL 823
Though their learning may be abundantly good,
ignoble men rarely learn goodness of heart.

KURAL 824
Fear the cunning friend who, harboring
wickedness in his heart, smiles sweetly to your face.

KURAL 825
Distrust whatever words may come from men
whose hearts do not beat in harmony with your own.

KURAL 826
Sounding very much like a good friend's words,
a rival's words are nonetheless known very quickly.

KURAL 827
Knowing how the bending of a bow forebodes nothing but harm,
never trust an enemy, though he bends low in his speech.

KURAL 828
Folded in respect, a foe's hands may hide a dagger.
So, too, his tears dare not be trusted.

KURAL 829
Men may amply aid you, yet despise you in their heart;
make them laugh, but let feigned friendship die.

KURAL 830
When the time comes that foes pose as friends,
keep a friendly face but banish their brotherhood from your heart.

பேதைமை என்பதொன்று யாதெனின் ஏதங்கொண்டு
ஊதியம் போக விடல்.

Folly

KURAL 831

What is folly? It is holding on to that which is harmful
and throwing away that which is helpful.

KURAL 832

The folly of all follies is to find pleasure in
doing what one is forbidden to do.

KURAL 833

To be shameless, uninquisitive, loveless and uncaring
are four failings common among all fools.

KURAL 834

No fool is more foolish than one who eagerly expounds
his learning to others while failing to follow it himself.

KURAL 835

It only takes a single birth for a fool to earn by his efforts
a morass of misery in the succeeding seven births.

KURAL 836

Not knowing how to act, when a fool undertakes an enterprise,
he doesn't just fail, he shackles himself in chains.

KURAL 837

Should a fool fall upon a great fortune,
strangers will feast while his family starves.

KURAL 838

If a fool happens to acquire something of value,
he will behave like a drunken lunatic.

KURAL 839

Friendship among fools is particularly sweet,
for there is not the slightest pain when they part.

KURAL 840

A fool's stepping into a saintly council
is like entering a clean bed with filthy feet.

Ignorance

KURAL 841

Dearth of wisdom is the direst destitution.
Other poverties the world deems less impoverishing.

KURAL 842

If any merit is gained when a fool gives a gift, however gladly,
it is due to the recipient's past penance and nothing else.

KURAL 843

The suffering that ignorant men inflict upon themselves
can hardly be contrived by their enemies.

KURAL 844

What is stupidity, you ask? It is the conceit
that dares to declare, "I am wise."

KURAL 845

He who pretends to knowledge he does not possess
raises doubts about the things he really knows.

KURAL 846

Fools follow a perverse path, clothing their well-formed naked body,
yet never thinking to conceal their deformed mind.

KURAL 847

Neglecting valuable advice, an ignorant man
becomes the cause of his own misery.

KURAL 848

That soul who neither follows another's orders nor fathoms what to
do himself creates nothing but torment until he leaves this life.

KURAL 849

As an unseeing man sees only the ways of his own mind, whoever
attempts to open the eyes of those who will not see is himself blind.

KURAL 850

He who denies as false what the world declares
to be true is deemed to be an earthly demon.

பகல்கருதிப் பற்றா
செயினும் இகல்கருதி
இன்னாசெய் யாமை தலை.

Hatred

KURAL 851

It is said that hatred is the disease that spreads
the plagues of discord among all living creatures.

KURAL 852

Though men devise disunity and deliberately harm you,
the highest path plots no hateful retribution.

KURAL 853

Removing the incurable cancer called hatred
reveals one's immortal, undiminishing splendor.

KURAL 854

The quelling of hatred, that sorrow of sorrows,
confers on man the joy of joys.

KURAL 855

Who is there who can conquer those
who have relinquished all hostilities?

KURAL 856

For all who boast that they take delight in hatred,
failure and death are drawing near.

KURAL 857

Men filled with hatred, knowingly causing harm to others,
never see that their hoped-for triumph lies in God's true grace.

KURAL 858

Wealth increases when a man walks away from hatred
and diminishes whenever he draws it near.

KURAL 859

Seeing a prosperous season approach, men neglect hatred.
In times of ruin, they nurture it lavishly.

KURAL 860

Out of hatred springs all bitter suffering,
while cheerful friendship yields good fortune's every joy.

செறுவார்க்குச் சேணிகவா
இன்பம் அறிவிலா
அஞ்சும் பகைவர்ப் பெறின்

The Merits of Enmity

KURAL 861

Rein in antagonism against the strong,
but unleash animosity against feeble adversaries.

KURAL 862

How can an unloving man, with neither powerful allies
nor the strength to stand alone, overcome mighty enemies?

KURAL 863

He who is fearful, ignorant, unfriendly and uncharitable
proves an easy prey to his enemies.

KURAL 864

Letting go of his secrets but not his antipathy,
a man becomes easy prey to anyone, anywhere, anytime.

KURAL 865

Without character, conscience, piety and propriety,
a man may yet be delightful—to his enemies!

KURAL 866

Even hatred can be a welcome thing, when it comes from
scoundrels seized by blind rage and indulgent lust.

KURAL 867

Some men undertake a task, then undermine it unawares.
Acquire their hatred—indeed, pay good money for it.

KURAL 868

If a man has no virtues and many vices, he will surely have
no allies, and this will be his enemies' surest advantage.

KURAL 869

Finding that his foe is ignorant and afraid to fight,
the attacker's cheerfulness cannot forsake him.

KURAL 870

Fame will flee the grasp of one who fails to grasp
the wealth of an enemy who is angry and unlearned.

இளந்தாக முள்மரம் கொல்க கிளையுநர்
கைகொல்லும் காழத்த இடத்து.

Understanding the Nature of Enmity

KURAL 871

So accursed is the thing called hatred that one
should never wish for it—even in jest.

KURAL 872

It is bad enough to incur the enmity of those who live by the bow,
but never provoke the hatred of those who sow and reap with words.

KURAL 873

One man who, all by himself, arouses hatred in many
is crazier than any lunatic.

KURAL 874

The world abides beneath the greatness
of noble-natured rulers who befriend even their enemies.

KURAL 875

Finding that he faces two foes and has no allies,
a lone man lures one to side with him.

KURAL 876

When distress dawns, neither draw near nor depart from
new friends and foes—rather, leave them alone.

KURAL 877

Never tell your troubles to those who cannot comprehend them,
nor expose your weaknesses to your enemies.

KURAL 878

Engineer a plan, execute that plan well and ensure
your security—thus is the joy of rivals forever ruined.

KURAL 879

Chop down a thorny tree while it is young.
Left to grow mature, it will one day cut the cutter's hand.

KURAL 880

Those who fail to quell a hostile rival's pride
will be blown away by the mere fact that he still breathes.

உடம்பாடு இலாதவர் வாழ்க்கை குடங்கருள்
பாம்போடு உடனுறைந் தற்று.

Internal Enmity

KURAL 881

Even shade and water are unpleasant if they breed disease.
So, too, may relatives be unpleasant if they cause harm.

KURAL 882

Fear not the foe who is like a drawn sword;
rather fear the friendship of an enemy who poses as kin.

KURAL 883

Dread hatred from within and defend yourself against it.
In calamitous times it will cut deeper than a potter's knife.

KURAL 884

Hidden hatreds may lurk only in the mind,
yet among kin they can manifest many miseries.

KURAL 885

Hate hidden in a kinsman's heart will cause
many miseries, and more—it will kill a man.

KURAL 886

When hatred arises, dissension destroys unity,
and men fall inescapably toward ever-ready death.

KURAL 887

A house that harbors hatred will never be a united whole,
though, like a vessel and its lid, it may appear to be one.

KURAL 888

As iron is worn away by frequent filing,
a family's strength is eroded by incessant inner frictions.

KURAL 889

Internal dissension may seem as small as a split sesame seed,
yet there is enough power in it to destroy.

KURAL 890

Living with those who cannot dwell in harmony
is like living in a hut with a deadly cobra.

ஏற்றிய கொள்கையார் சீற்றின் இடைமுறிந்து
வேந்தனும் வேந்து கெடும்.

Not Offending the Great

KURAL 891

Of all the ways to protect oneself, the foremost is this:
do not belittle the prowess of powerful men.

KURAL 892

Disrespectful conduct toward great men will bring,
through those great men, unremitting miseries.

KURAL 893

If you desire destruction, simply ignore the rules
and provoke those who, if they desire, can destroy you.

KURAL 894

For the powerless to wreak harm upon the powerful
is to summon Death with a gesturing hand.

KURAL 895

Once he incurs a fierce king's withering wrath,
one is doomed, wherever he wanders, whatever he does.

KURAL 896

Though burned by a blazing fire, one may still survive;
but there is no survival for those who offend great men.

KURAL 897

What is the use of a man's varied life and splendid wealth
if he reaps the wrath of great and righteous men?

KURAL 898

If men of mountainous stature are meagerly esteemed,
others who seemed as enduring as earth will die, as will their kin.

KURAL 899

The most kingly king will tumble from his throne and die,
should he unleash a towering sage's bridled temper.

KURAL 900

Though he commands unrivaled powers of protection,
a king cannot survive the wrath of powerful ascetics.

இல்லாளை அஞ்சுவான் அஞ்சுமற் றெஞ்ஞான்றும்
நல்லார்க்கு நல்ல செயல்.

Being Led by Women

KURAL 901
Men who dote upon their wives never achieve great gains,
and men of great ambition avoid that very thing.

KURAL 902
The riches of a man who fawningly follows a woman's lead
will buy him only shameful shame.

KURAL 903
An abnormal submissiveness to his spouse
will earn a man endless disgrace among decent men.

KURAL 904
Though he has mastered the doing of deeds,
the henpecked husband merits little in this life or the next.

KURAL 905
A man's fears of his own wife will make him
constantly fearful of doing good for good folks.

KURAL 906
Though providence has filled his life,
a man who fears his graceful spouse is devoid of dignity.

KURAL 907
A woman's shy ways show great dignity,
unlike a man who lives to do a woman's bidding.

KURAL 908
Those who live only to fulfill their wive's wishes
can neither satisfy the needs of friends nor benefit others.

KURAL 909
Neither virtuous deeds nor vast wealth nor domestic joys
will be found with men who carry out their wife's commands.

KURAL 910
Moneyed men whose thoughts dwell in the mind
never dwell foolishly on relationships with women.

பொருட்பெண்டிர் பொய்ம்மை முயக்கம் இருட்டறையில்
ஏதில் பிணந்தழீ இ யற்று.

Wanton Women

KURAL 911

The sweet words of beautifully bangled women who desire
a man's wealth and not his love decree his fall into disgrace.

KURAL 912

Weigh the worth and abandon the company of wanton women
who, weighing their profit, prattle about their virtues.

KURAL 913

A mercenary woman pretends intimate embrace,
but in the darkened room, she caresses a stranger's carcass.

KURAL 914

Men seeking spiritual treasures are too worldly wise
to touch tawdry women who treasure only material riches.

KURAL 915

Men of innate good sense and acquired wisdom
never touch tramps who shamelessly share their beauty with all.

KURAL 916

Desiring to maintain their jubilant goodness, men will not
embrace enticing women who proffer lewd charms to all.

KURAL 917

Only men of unchaste mind will lie in the arms of women
whose hearts chase after other things as they embrace.

KURAL 918

It is said that men devoid of discerning wisdom
succumb to a deceiving damsel's embrace as to a siren's song.

KURAL 919

The soft arms of the elegantly bejeweled harlot
are a murky mire that engulfs wicked, stupid men.

KURAL 920

Two-faced females, besotting brew and addictive dice
befriend the men whom fortune has forsaken.

துஞ்சினார் செத்தாரின் வேரல்லர் எஞ்ஞான்றும் நஞ்சுண்பார் கள்ளுண் பவர்.

Avoidance of Drunkenness

KURAL 921

Those who crave intoxicating drink each day
will never be feared and never find fame.

KURAL 922

Do not drink liquor. If some wish to, let it be those
who have no wish for the esteem of exemplary men.

KURAL 923

The sight of a drunken man's revelry is unbearable
even to his own mother. How, then, must it appear to the wise?

KURAL 924

The virtuous damsel called Decency will turn her back
on men who indulge in the vile vice called drunkenness.

KURAL 925

Spending one's wealth to purchase self-oblivion
results from being oblivious to proper conduct.

KURAL 926

Those who always sleep are akin to the dead.
Those who constantly drink are like men who take poison.

KURAL 927

The drooping eyes of those who secretly drink betray that secret,
evoking their neighbor's relentless ridicule.

KURAL 928

Stop denying, "I never drink," for next time you drink,
your mind's hidden deception will be betrayed then and there.

KURAL 929

One may as well carry a candle under water to search for
a drowned man as use reason to sober a drunk drowned in drink.

KURAL 930

Why can't the drunkard who, when sober, sees another's drunken
stupor realize the degrading shame of his own drunkenness?

கவறும் கழகமும் கையும் தருக்கி
இவரியார் இல்லாகி யார்

Gambling

KURAL 931

Do not take to gambling, even if you can win,
for your wins will be like the baited hooks that fish swallow.

KURAL 932

To win once, a gambler loses a hundred times.
What a way to procure happiness and prosperity!

KURAL 933

Incessantly calling bets on rolling dice causes
a man's rich reserves and potential revenues to run elsewhere.

KURAL 934

Gambling brings on many miseries and erodes one's good name.
Nothing else ends in such wretched poverty.

KURAL 935

Desiring to win everything, those who love the dice,
the gambling hall and their lucky hand lose it all.

KURAL 936

Gambling is Misfortune's other name. Fools ensnared by her
will suffer an empty stomach and distressing sorrows.

KURAL 937

Spending time in the gambling hall squanders
ancestral wealth and wastes personal worth.

KURAL 938

Gambling will consume a man's wealth and corrupt his honesty.
It will curtail his benevolence and increase his torment.

KURAL 939

Those who take to gambling's fickle gain forfeit these five:
raiments, riches, rations, renown and erudition.

KURAL 940

The gambler's passion increases with the losses incurred.
Even so does the soul's craving for life grow with the griefs suffered.

உற்றவன் தீர்ப்பான் மருந்துழைச்
செல்வானென்று
அப்பால்நாற் கூற்றே மருந்து.

Medicine

KURAL 941
Disease is but deficiency or excess of three life forces,
defined by writers of scientific texts as air, fire and water.

KURAL 942
The body requires no medicine if you eat
only after the food you have already eaten is digested.

KURAL 943
Once digestion is complete, eat with moderation;
that is the way to prolong the life of the body.

KURAL 944
Assured the last meal has digested and sensing a keen appetite,
savor only foods that are fully agreeable.

KURAL 945
Life remains unharmed when one eats with restraint,
refraining from foods that have proven disagreeable.

KURAL 946
The pleasures of health abide in the man who eats moderately.
The pains of disease dwell with him who eats excessively.

KURAL 947
The thoughtless glutton who gorges himself beyond the limits
of his digestive fires will be consumed by limitless ills.

KURAL 948
Diagnose the illness, trace its cause,
seek the appropriate remedy and apply it skillfully.

KURAL 949
An accomplished doctor prescribes a remedy after considering
the patient's nature, the disease's nature and the time of year.

KURAL 950
Medicine consists of a patient, a physician, a prescription
and a nurse—each of these having four parts.

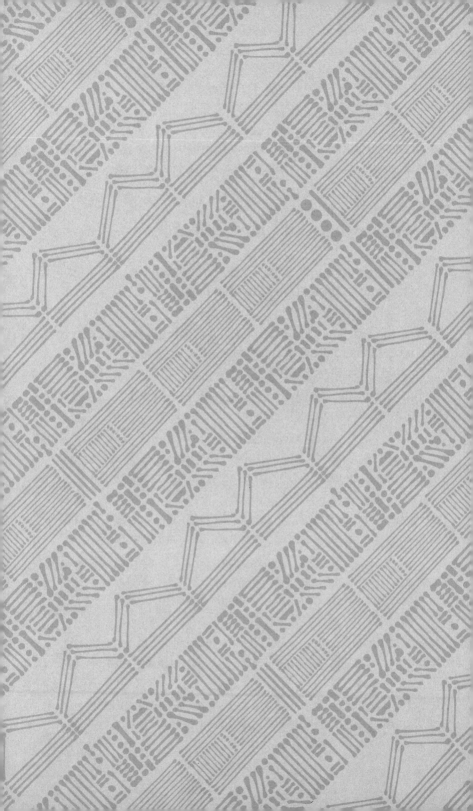

Olipiyal
ஒழிபியல்

நிலத்திற் கிடந்தமை கால்காட்டும், காட்டும்
குலத்திற் பிறந்தார்வாய்ச் சொல்.

Appendix

The nature of a soil is known by the seedlings that it sprouts.
The nature of a man's family is known by the words he speaks.

T HE LAST SECTION OF *WEAVER'S WISDOM* IS SIMPLY
       ABOUT THE QUALITIES OF PEOPLE. IT IS SOMEWHAT
       OF A WHO'S WHO OF MANKIND. HAVE YOU EVER
wondered about the qualities of the noble? Have you ever
wondered about bad money and good money? Have you ever,
in your secret thoughts, had the desire to surround yourself
with the best of people, not knowing how you found yourself
in the midst of disappointments and surprises? Choosing
proper friends is more important than choosing an automo-
bile or the furniture to surround yourself with in your home
or office. There is a great difference between friends and acquaintances. In today's world this is not well understood.
Reading these thirteen chapters will shed a great deal of light
on who is who among relatives, friends and acquaintances.

Everyone today, in one way or another, is wanting to improve themselves. In the verses of this section we find simple,
not-to-be-disputed guidelines. Wondering whom to vote for out
of a display of contenders for governmental office? Advice in
abundance is all here to read, understand, absorb and put into
action for a better life for the individual and community.

The weaver has no mercy when he speaks of the preservation of honor—no mercy at all. And he extols greatness. Greatness and accomplishment are what the first gurus of a youth,
the parents, should impart. Yes, everyone has a guru. The
world itself is the teacher of most people living on the planet,
for they have no other mentor, nor even want one. I call this
great guru, the world, Sri Sri Sri Vishvaguru Maha-Maharaj,
and he teaches his followers to learn by their own mistakes.
By following the weaver's wisdom, we can circumvent Vishvaguru and avoid the many errors, mishaps and sorrows he
uses as teaching tools for learning painful lessons.

What is needed today more than anything else, in the
home, in the village, among leaders and followers, is what is
explained to the nth degree in chapter 100. This can be read

time and again, memorized, then put into daily practice. Offering a new angle on courtesy, the weaver talks of what we know so well happens in most homes: "Disparaging words are painful, even when uttered in jest. Hence, knowers of human nature are courteous even to enemies."

In the ancient days of the Tamil people, modesty prevailed in personal relations, and it was extolled in poems, songs, paintings and architecture. Today modesty is regarded among these amazing people as a treasure more valuable than a treasury of gold and jewels. Modesty, a good family and well-chosen friends of proven loyalty are the crosswise threads that crisscross the warp as life's patterns unfold. Remember, if there are troubles in the family, which is a group brought together because of past karmas that cannot be erased, it is crucial for family members to huddle and take care of, support, one another against internal turmoil and the onslaughts of the world. To harbor resentment against mother, father, brother, sister or close and distant relatives is to weaken the fabric of one's life. It would be like stringing a loom with strong, taut, lengthwise threads interspersed with weak, breakable ones. Then the colorful, crisscross threads, dark and bright, of life's experiences would produce an emotionally disturbing pattern, and the fabric would not be smooth to the touch, but frail and rough in spots, prone to tear and break when stressed. Today this is called a discouraged family.

The wise old weaver has taken us on a great journey, giving us a loom on which to weave our life to our heart's content. He begins with the greatest God, ends with the lowest of men and covers everything in between. Quite an achievement, I would say, for a mere 1,080 verses inscribed on palm leaves 2,200 years ago for us to live up to today.

அடுக்கிய கோடி பெறினும் குடிப்பிறந்தார்
குன்றுவ செய்தல் இலர்.

Nobility

KURAL 951
An innate sense of right and shying away from wrong
are found together only in the nobly born.

KURAL 952
Men of noble birth will never fall away from these three:
correct conduct, truthfulness and modesty.

KURAL 953
Four traits define the true gentleman: a smiling face,
a generous hand, a courteous demeanor and kindly words.

KURAL 954
Though millions upon millions could be gained by it,
men nobly born would never commit a demeaning deed.

KURAL 955
Though their means of charitableness may be cut off,
venerable families will never be severed from propriety.

KURAL 956
Those committed to their family's flawless fame
dare not commit deceitful, dishonorable deeds.

KURAL 957
In high-born men, blemishes are clearly seen,
just as the moon's elevation makes it more visible.

KURAL 958
When a man with good background lacks loving affection,
doubts arise whether he arose from that family.

KURAL 959
The nature of a soil is known by the seedlings it sprouts.
The nature of a man's family is known by the words he speaks.

KURAL 960
Those desiring greatness must desire modesty. Those seeking
their family's honor must seek to be respectful to all.

பெருக்கத்து வேண்டும் பணிதல் சிறிய
சுருக்கத்து வேண்டும் உயர்வு.

Honor

KURAL 961

Shun any actions that will diminish honor,
even if they are vital for the preservation of life.

KURAL 962

Those who honorably pursue glory never act ingloriously,
even if glorious fame is to be gained.

KURAL 963

Cultivate modesty in the midst of good fortune,
but in times of adversity preserve your dignity.

KURAL 964

Honorable men fallen from high status
are like useless hair fallen from the head.

KURAL 965

Unworthy acts, though mustard-seed small, will bring down
a man, though he towers like a mountain.

KURAL 966

It offers neither Earth's renown nor Heaven's refuge,
so why do men run after and stand by those who revile them?

KURAL 967

Better to die right where you stand, the saying goes,
than to live running after those who despise you.

KURAL 968

Will any medicine preserve the body of the high-born man
whose honor has already perished?

KURAL 969

Shorn of its hair, the yak will refuse to live.
Such men do exist who prefer death to the loss of honor.

KURAL 970

The world will extol and exalt honorable men
who exult in death rather than endure dishonor.

மேலிருந்தும் மேலல்லார் மேலல்லர் கீழிருந்தும்
கீழல்லார் கீழல் லவர்.

Greatness

KURAL 971

The aspiration for glorious achievement is the light of life.
Disgrace is the dark thought that says, "I can live without it."

KURAL 972

All men who live are alike at birth.
Diverse actions define their distinction and distinctiveness.

KURAL 973

Lowly men are never high, even when elevated.
High souls are never low, even when downtrodden.

KURAL 974

Like chastity in a woman, greatness is guarded
by being true to one's own self.

KURAL 975

A man possessing greatness possesses the power
to effectively perform uncommonly difficult deeds.

KURAL 976

"We will befriend great men and become like them."
Such thoughts seldom intrude upon small minds.

KURAL 977

When small-minded men do achieve some distinction,
it only serves to augment their arrogance.

KURAL 978

Greatness is always humbly self-effacing,
while pettiness adorns itself with words of praise.

KURAL 979

Greatness abides in the absence of arrogance.
Smallness proudly parades its fulsome haughtiness.

KURAL 980

Greatness conceals by silence the weaknesses of others.
Pettiness promptly proclaims such things to all.

அன்புநாண் ஒப்புரவு
கண்ணோட்டம் வாய்மையொடு
ஐந்துசால் ஊன்றிய தூண்.

Perfect Goodness

KURAL 981

It is said that all good things are natural to those
who know their duty and walk the path of perfect goodness.

KURAL 982

Perfect men hold as good their own good character.
They count no other goodness so genuinely good.

KURAL 983

Love, modesty, propriety, a kindly eye and truthfulness—
these are the five pillars on which perfect goodness rests.

KURAL 984

Penance is the goodness that refrains utterly from killing.
Perfection is the goodness that refuses to utter others' faults.

KURAL 985

Humility is the strength of the strong
and the instrument the wise use to reform their foes.

KURAL 986

The touchstone of perfect character is
accepting with dignity defeat from one's inferiors.

KURAL 987

Of what gain is perfect goodness if it does not do good to all,
even to those who have done painful things to others?

KURAL 988

Deprived of all else, one remains undisgraced
if still endowed with strength of character.

KURAL 989

Destiny's last days may surge with oceanic change,
yet perfectly good men remain, like the shore, unchanged.

KURAL 990

Should the perfect virtue of perfect men ever diminish,
this mighty Earth would bear our burdensome weight no more.

எண்பதத்தால் எய்தல் எளிதென்ப யார்மாட்டும்
பண்புடைமை என்னும் வழக்கு.

Possession of Courtesy

KURAL 991
They say if a man is easily accessible to everyone,
the virtue of courtesy will be easily accessible to him.

KURAL 992
Loving kindness and birth in a good family—
these two are said to confer on one a gracious manner.

KURAL 993
Resemblance among humans is not that their bodies look alike.
Real similarities come from similar traits of courtesy.

KURAL 994
The world commends the civility of those
who combine fruitful effort and kindly benevolence.

KURAL 995
Disparaging words are painful even when uttered in jest.
Hence, knowers of human nature are courteous even to enemies.

KURAL 996
The world exists because civilized men exist.
Without them, it would collapse into mere dust.

KURAL 997
Though their minds are as sharp as a wood rasp,
men without human decency are as wooden as a tree.

KURAL 998
It is disgraceful to be discourteous towards others,
even to unfriendly fellows who treat you unjustly.

KURAL 999
To those who cannot smile in joy, this wide world
lies engulfed in darkness, even in broad daylight.

KURAL 1000
Great wealth amassed by men who lack sweet courtesy
is like good milk turned sour in an unclean vessel.

வைத்தான்வாய் சான்ற பெரும்பொருள் அஃதுண்ணான்
செத்தான் செயக்கிடந்தது இல்.

Wealth That Benefits No One

KURAL 1001
He who has amassed great wealth but does not enjoy it
is reckoned as dead, like his unused heap.

KURAL 1002
Believing wealth is everything, yet giving away nothing,
the miser himself will be possessed by a miserable birth.

KURAL 1003
The mere sight of men who lust after wealth,
caring nothing for renown, is a burden to the Earth.

KURAL 1004
What could a man, unloved by even a single soul,
imagine he might leave to posterity?

KURAL 1005
Amid millions heaped high, a man remains poor
if he neither gives away his wealth nor enjoys it himself.

KURAL 1006
Vast wealth can be a wretched curse to one who
neither gladdens himself in its worth nor gives to the worthy.

KURAL 1007
The wealth of a greedy man who gives nothing to the needy
is like the beauty of a maiden growing old unwed.

KURAL 1008
The wealth of a man whom no heart loves
is like fruits on a poisonous tree in the heart of a village.

KURAL 1009
He who casts out love and dharma and chooses self-denial
so wealth can pile high will see it seized by strangers.

KURAL 1010
The short-lived poverty of a benevolent rich man
is like the temporary dryness of a bountiful rain cloud.

கருமத்தால் நாணுதல் நாணுந் திருவுடையல்
நல்லவர் நாணுப் பிற.

Possession of Modesty

KURAL 1011
For fair-faced maidens, modesty means bashfulness,
but the deeper modesty shies away from shameful karmas.

KURAL 1012
Food, clothing and such do not differ much among people;
what distinguishes good men from others is modesty.

KURAL 1013
All life clings to a body;
perfect goodness clings to all that is modest.

KURAL 1014
Is not modesty a jewel adorning perfect men?
Without it, is not their strut an awful blemish to behold?

KURAL 1015
The world decrees that men who are as ashamed
by others' disgrace as by their own are modesty's fondest home.

KURAL 1016
The great would rather hold themselves behind
modesty's barricade than breach it to acquire the vast world.

KURAL 1017
Those who prize unpretentiousness will forsake life to preserve it.
But they never forsake modesty for the sake of life.

KURAL 1018
If a man does not feel ashamed of what makes others feel ashamed,
virtue itself will be ashamed of him.

KURAL 1019
Failing to observe good conduct, one sets his family on fire.
Living in shamelessness, he incinerates everything good.

KURAL 1020
The movements of men devoid of modesty mock life,
like wooden puppets suspended on a string.

கருமம் செயஒருவன் கைதூவேன் என்னும்
பெருமையின் பீடுடையது இல்.

Advancing the Community

KURAL 1021

No greater dignity exists than when a man resolutely declares,
"I will never cease in laboring to fulfill my karmas."

KURAL 1022

One prolongs his clan by prolonged exertion in
both perseverance and sound understanding.

KURAL 1023

When a man vows to advance his community,
God Himself will wrap His robes and lead the way.

KURAL 1024

When a man's effort to raise his community high is unremitting,
his work will prosper on its own, even if he makes no plans.

KURAL 1025

The world will surround and befriend him
who, without fault, lives to advance his community.

KURAL 1026

It is said that true manliness consists in becoming
head and provider of the clan one was born into.

KURAL 1027

As on a battlefield the burden falls upon the brave,
in the community weight is carried by the most competent.

KURAL 1028

Those seeking to improve their clan await no season,
for delays and undue regard for dignity will destroy it.

KURAL 1029

When a man shields his family from every suffering,
doesn't his body become a vessel filled with their afflictions?

KURAL 1030

Without good men to hold it up, the family home will fall
the moment misfortune's axe comes down.

சுழன்றும்ஏர்ப்
பின்னது உலகம்
அதனால் உழந்தும் உழவே தலை.

Farming

KURAL 1031

Wherever it may wander, the world follows the farmer's plow.
Thus despite all its hardships, farming is the foremost occupation.

KURAL 1032

Farmers are the linchpin of the world, for they support all
who take up other work, not having the strength to plow.

KURAL 1033

Those who live by the plow live in self-sufficiency.
All others lean on them to simply subsist.

KURAL 1034

Those whose fields lie shaded by abundant sheaves of grain
will see many nations overshadowed by their own.

KURAL 1035

Those who eat food harvested with their own hands
will never beg and never refuse a beggar's outstretched palm.

KURAL 1036

When plowers of the fields stand idly with folded arms,
even desireless ascetics will not last long.

KURAL 1037

If soil is dried so that one ounce shrinks to one-quarter ounce,
fruitful yields will not require a single handful of fertilizer.

KURAL 1038

It is better to fertilize than to furrow a field. After weeding,
it is more important to watch over a field than even to water it.

KURAL 1039

If the lord of the land fails to visit his fields,
they will sulk as surely as a neglected wife.

KURAL 1040

Mother Earth laughs when she sees
lazy men crying, "We are so poor."

நெருப்பினுள் துஞ்சலும் ஆகும் நிரப்பினுள்
யாதொன்றும் கண்பாடு அரிது.

Poverty

KURAL 1041

Ask what is more miserable than being poor,
and the answer comes—only poverty pains like poverty.

KURAL 1042

Poverty, the cruelest of demons, deprives a man
of every joy in this life, then takes them from the next life.

KURAL 1043

Craving, another name for poverty, will obliterate at once
ancestral honor and dignity of speech.

KURAL 1044

Privation produces unmindfulness, which gives birth
to improper words, even in men of proper birth.

KURAL 1045

Poverty is that single sorrow which
gives rise to a multitude of miseries.

KURAL 1046

Even when the poor perceive profoundly and speak skillfully,
their most meaningful words are always forgotten.

KURAL 1047

He who is impoverished and estranged from virtue will be
regarded as a stranger even by his own mother.

KURAL 1048

Will the wretched poverty that nearly
killed me yesterday come again today?

KURAL 1049

Men may slumber even in the midst of fire,
but none can find repose in the midst of poverty.

KURAL 1050

Lacking a morsel of food, a man may either
slay every desire or kill off his neighbor's salt and rice broth.

இரத்தலும் ஈதலே போலும் காத்தல்
கனவிலும் தேற்றாதார் மாட்டு.

Begging

KURAL 1051

If you meet a man of means, by all means beg his help.
If he refuses, the fault is his, not yours.

KURAL 1052

Even begging can prove pleasurable
when what is begged for comes with no sense of burden.

KURAL 1053

Begging has its own beauty when one supplicates
before dutiful men whose hearts never say no.

KURAL 1054

There are men who never deny a request, even in their dreams.
Begging from them is the same as giving.

KURAL 1055

Because men do exist on Earth who never begrudge giving,
others dare to plead their needs before men's gaze.

KURAL 1056

The miseries of begging will flee at the mere sight
of those who are free from refusal's miserable manners.

KURAL 1057

A jubilant heart rejoices upon seeing
those who give without scoffing or scorning.

KURAL 1058

Deprived of beggars, this vast and verdant Earth would
become uncharitable, a ball for the play of wooden puppets.

KURAL 1059

What glory would generous men enjoy
if there were none to beg for and receive their gifts?

KURAL 1060

One who begs and is refused should not be angry,
for his own poverty is sufficient proof of giving's limits.

இரவுள்ள உள்ளம் உருகும் கரவுள்ள
உள்ளதூஉம் இன்றிக் கெடும்.

Dread of Begging

KURAL 1061

It is ten million times better not to beg, even from those
precious men whose joy is giving and who thus never refuse.

KURAL 1062

Were it the World-Creator's wish for men to live by begging,
men might wish that He, too, die a wandering beggar.

KURAL 1063

There is no greater foolhardiness than to say,
"I shall end the pains of poverty by begging."

KURAL 1064

This entire world is too small to contain the dignity of men
who will not stoop to beg, even in the direst destitution.

KURAL 1065

Though it is only gruel, thin as water, nothing is more savory
than food that is earned by the labor of one's own hands.

KURAL 1066

The tongue finds nothing more distasteful than begging,
even just to beg drinking water for a cow.

KURAL 1067

This I beg of all beggars:
"If you must beg, beg not from misers."

KURAL 1068

The unsturdy ship called begging will break apart
the moment it crashes against the rock of refusal.

KURAL 1069

Thoughts of a beggar's plight melt the heart.
Thoughts of refusals he receives crush it completely.

KURAL 1070

Having said "no" to a beggar, knowing it might kill the poor man,
where is a miser going to hide from his word?

அறைபறை அன்னர் கயவர்தாம்கேட்ட
மறைபிறர்க்கு உய்த்துரைக்க லான்.

Baseness

KURAL 1071

Outwardly, vile men resemble human beings.
We have never witnessed such a remarkable likeness.

KURAL 1072

The low-minded are happier than men who know goodness,
for they are never troubled by the pangs of conscience.

KURAL 1073

Wicked rogues resemble the Gods,
for they, too, live doing whatever they want.

KURAL 1074

When a vile man meets a wicked one, he will outdo him
in his vices and pride himself on the achievement.

KURAL 1075

Fear is the primary force motivating base men.
Besides that, the desire for gain may motivate them—a little.

KURAL 1076

Base men are like a bass drum, sounding off
to others every secret they happen to hear.

KURAL 1077

Some men are too crude to even shake the water off their just-washed
hands, except for those who could break their jaw with a fist.

KURAL 1078

Worthy men yield their gifts when told of a need, but like sugarcane,
base men give only when crushed and squeezed.

KURAL 1079

Let a base man behold others dressing and dining well,
and instantly their faults are all that he can see.

KURAL 1080

Is there anything for which lowly men are suited? Well,
when crises come, they are the first to offer themselves for sale!

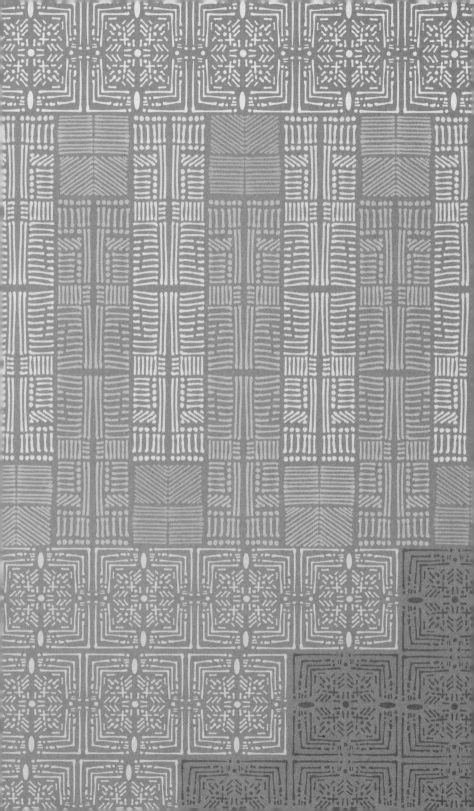

Conclusion

Mutiverai

முடிவுரை

W E HAVE TAKEN GREAT PLEASURE IN PRESENTING THIS EDITION TO THE WORLD OF SEEKERS FOR A BETTER LIFE. HEEDING THE WISDOM HEREIN IS A dharma that has been tried and tested century after century. after century. Decision-making in planning the future and understanding the past while living in the present is made easy through these 1,080 verses. All who look to India as the land of spirituality will find here the best of the East augmenting the best of the West, making a wholesome whole in claiming the weaver's wisdom as their own lifestyle. There is a new age ahead, and we are certain that the Tamil people, and those who have chosen to live as they once lived, will take a needed and welcome lead. We here at our Hawaiian ashram base our decisions, which are many and made daily, upon the weaver's precepts. By doing so, a concise and precise governing body, otherwise imperceptible, gives consistent advice to followers worldwide. As the hereditary guru of the Jaffna Tamil community of Sri Lanka—now in diaspora as refugees flee because of war—my decisions for community welfare and future development made on the *Tirukural's* understanding of dharma keep decision-making consistent with priests and elders in over twenty nations where we have established temples and encouraged traditional ways of worship and culture. For a new age to really be a new age, two things must happen: first, spiritual leaders must be strong enough to influence community leaders by example and unfailing advice; and second, corporal punishment must end and harmony must exist in every school and home.

Glossary

Sollakaraati
சொல்லகராதி

𝔄*adheenam*: ஆதீனம் "Ownership, possession, dependence; endowment, foundation, institution;" Saiva monastery. A Saivite Hindu monastery-temple complex in the South Indian, Saiva Siddhanta tradition. The *aadheenam* head, or pontiff, is called the *Guru Mahasannidhanam* or *aadheenakartar,* who traditionally consecrates the scepter of the *maharaja* through sacred ceremony. See: *Hinduism, Śaiva Siddhanta, sannidhanam.*

abide: To live or remain in a place; to endure or dwell.

abound: To exist in great numbers or quantity. —**to abound in:** to have in great numbers or quantity.

Abrahamic religions: The three religions: Judaism, Christianity and Islam, which descend from the lineage of Abraham, originating in the Middle East. They are all based in the Biblical tradition, which holds that God and man are eternally separate.

accessible: Easy to approach.

accumulate: To amass, cause to accrue, or gather.

accursed: Under a curse; doomed and ill-fated.

achieve: To accomplish or attain. —**achievement:** accomplishment or attainment.

acknowledge: Give recognition to; admit the truth or worth of.

acre: An area of land measuring 43,560 square feet (approx. 4047 square meters).

adage: A concisely stated truth. Proverb, maxim.

addiction: Enslavement to a habit. A medical condition in which one's body or mind has become dependent on the continually escalating use of or participation in a particular substance or activity.

addictive: Prone to be compulsively and physiologically dependent on a habit-forming substance, mental affliction, or a habitual life pattern, such as gambling, TV, pornography or other attraction, usually harmful in nature.

Adi Granth: आदिग्रन्थ "First book." The central Sikh scripture. Its eloquent teachings are in harmony with Hinduism, but for the rejection of the Vedas and disavowal of image worship and caste.

adjudicate: To hear and give judgment in a dispute or problem.

administrate: To manage, conduct or direct.

admonition: Advice or warning.

adorning: Decorating or beautifying through ornamentation.

adultery: Engaging in sexual relations with someone other than one's spouse.

adversary: An enemy, foe or opponent.

adversity: Misfortune, disaster, affliction, hardship, distress.

affection: Fondness; a gentle, tender, loving feeling.

affliction: Pain or suffering; distress, grief, adversity. The state of being afflicted or beset with troubles.

affluent: Wealthy, well-to-do.

agenda: List of things to be dealt with or accomplished.

aggrieve: To offend; cause injury or grief.

ahimsa: अहिंसा "Noninjury," nonviolence or nonhurtfulness. Refraining from causing harm to others, physically, mentally or emotionally. Ahimsa is the first and most important of the Hindu religious restraints *(yamas)*. It is the cardinal virtue upon which all others depend.

akin: Like, related to, or similar.

alcohol: An intoxicating and addictive substance, ingredient in distilled and fermented liquors.

Alexander the Great: King of ancient Macedonia who invaded (but failed to conquer) North-West India ca 326 BCE. His soldiers mutinied; many stayed and intermarried with Indians. Cultural interchanges influenced both civilizations.

alien: Foreign.

allay: To lessen or alleviate.

altar: A raised surface or other place used for presenting offerings in worship.

amass: To gather, collect, accumulate or hoard.

amaze: To astonish; to produce feelings of awe and wonderment.

amid: Surrounded by; among, in the middle of.

anava: God's veiling power that provides individualness, or separate ego, to each soul, making the soul seem apart and distinct from God and the universe.

anguish: Distress, pain, suffering—often mental.

anicham: அணிச்சம் A small, delicate flower which wilts upon being smelled.

animosity: Strong dislike, enmity, hatred.

annihilate: To destroy or demolish completely.

antagonism: Hostility, opposition.

antagonist: He who opposes one's efforts or plans; an adversary.

antipathy: Strong dislike or hatred, aversion.

antiquated: Obsolete; no longer in current use.

apt: Appropriate, fitting.

archeology: The study of ancient peoples and how they lived, based on excavation of material relics, buried cities, etc.

ardent: Eager, fervent, intense.

ardor: Eagerness, intense feeling or enthusiasm, passion.

aristocrat: A nobleman or member of the privileged, upper-class.

arrogance: Unjustified pride in oneself; haughtiness; a domineering manner.

artha: अर्थ Wealth.

ascend: To move upward, as toward the Source.

ascendant: In or approaching a position of superiority or greatest influence.

ascertaining: Determining; making certain, as by careful examination.

ascetic: A person who leads a life of contemplation and rigorous self-denial, shunning comforts and pleasures for religious purposes. See: *austerity, renunciate, monk.*

asceticism: A religious way of life that stresses self-denial and self-discipline as a means toward spiritual progress. See: *ascetic, austerity.*

aspiration: A strongly felt wish, or working toward a goal.

assuage: To lessen, pacify or calm.

assumption: A hypothesis or belief which is based on incomplete evidence.

astral: Of the subtle, nonphysical sphere (astral plane) which exists between the physical and causal planes.

astute: Shrewd, keen, penetrating, subtle, sagacious.

atman: आत्मन् "The soul; the breath; the principle of life and sensation." The soul in its entirety—as the soul body *(anandamaya kosa)* and its essence (Parashakti and Parasiva). One of Hinduism's most fundamental tenets is that we are the *atman,* not the physical body, emotions, external mind or personality. In Hindu scriptures, *atman* sometimes refers to the ego-personality, and its meaning must be determined according to context.

attitude: Disposition. State of mind. Manner of carrying oneself. Manner of acting, thinking or feeling which reveals one's disposition, opinions and beliefs.

augment: To enlarge or increase; to add to.

Aum: ॐ or ஓம் Often spelled *Om.* The mystic syllable of Hinduism, placed at the beginning of most sacred writings. As a *mantra,* it is pronounced *aw* (as in *law*), *oo* (as in *zoo*), *mm. Aum* is explained in the *Upanishads* as standing for the whole world and its parts, including past, present and future. It is from this primal vibration that all manifestation issues forth. *Aum* is the primary, or *mula mantra,* and often precedes other *mantras.* It may be safely used for chanting and *japa* by anyone of any religion. Its three letters represent the three worlds and the powers of creation, preservation and destruction. In common usage in several Indian languages, *aum* means "yes, verily" or "hail."

auspicious: Favorable, of good omen, foreboding well. One of the central concepts in Hindu life.

austere: Very simple, yogic; strict in self-discipline and self-denial. See: *ascetic.*

austerities: Spiritual disciplines; self-denials.

austerity: Self-denial and discipline, physical or mental, performed for various reasons including acquiring powers, attaining grace, conquering the instinctive nature and burning the seeds of past *karmas.* Ranging from simple deprivations, such as foregoing a meal, to severe disciplines, called *tapas,* such as always standing, never sitting or lying down, even for sleep. See: *ascetic.*

Auvaiyar: ஔவையார் A saint of Tamil Nadu (ca 200 BCE), a contemporary (some say the sister) of Saint Tiruvalluvar, devotee of Lord Ganesha and Karttikeya and one of the greatest literary figures in ancient India. As a young girl, she prayed to have her beauty removed so as not to be forced into marriage and thus be able to devote her full life to God. She was a great *bhakta* who wrote exquisite ethical works, some in aphoristic style and some in four-line verse. Her Tamil primer is studied by children to this day. A second Saint Auvaiyar may have lived in the ninth century.

avail (oneself of): To make effective use of.

avarice: Greed, covetousness; inordinate desire to obtain and hoard wealth.

avert: To turn aside, ward off or prevent.

awesome: Inspiring feelings of reverence and wonder; splendid or full of awe.

anish: To drive away, exile or expel.

barrage: A heavy and prolonged attack.

barren: Unproductive of results or gains; unprofitable.

base: Low-minded, mean, ignoble. Also, to do or decide on the basis of.

BCE: Abbreviation (equivalent to BC, "before Christ") for "before common era," referring to dating prior to the year one in the Western, or Gregorian calendar, now in universal secular use. See also *CE*.

bedrock: The solid underlying foundation.

befit: To be suitable to.

begrudge: To give reluctantly or unwillingly.

beholden: Obliged to feel grateful; owing thanks; indebted.

belie: To demonstrate the untruth of.

benevolence: The quality of being benevolent.

benevolent: Benign, beneficent, generous, kind-hearted, philanthropic.

bereft: Deprived of, or lacking.

besotting: Stupefying, intoxicating, inebriating.

betrothed: The person whom one has a mutual pledge to marry.

bhakta: भक्त (Tamil: *Bhaktar.*) "Devotee." A worshiper. One who is surrendered to the Divine.

bias: Mental inclination or partiality.

bija: बीज "The seed." Semen is the essence of life, the purest form of the sacrificial-elixir (soma). *—bija mantra:* बीजमन्त्र "Seed syllable." A Sanskrit sound associated with a specific Deity used for invocation during mystic rites.

billowing: Large and swelling in mass.

bounty: Rewards; riches; goodness.

Brahma Sutra(s): ब्रह्मसूत्र Also known as the *Vedanta Sutras*, composed by Badarayana (perhaps as early as ca 400 BCE) as the first known systematic exposition of Upanishadic thought. Its 550 aphorisms are so brief as to be virtually unintelligible without commentary.

Brahmaloka: See: *Sivaloka.*

brahmin (brahmana): ब्राह्मन "Mature or evolved soul." The class of pious souls of exceptional learning. From *Brahman,* "growth, expansion, evolution, development, swelling of the spirit or soul." The mature soul is the exemplar of wisdom, tolerance, forbearance and humility.

brevity: Shortness, conciseness, succinctness.

bribe: Something, such as money or a favor, offered or given to a person in a position of trust to influence that person's views or conduct.

bridled: Restrained, governed, controlled. In context, to control one's expression of his otherwise voluminous unexpressed thoughts. (From "bridle," a head-harness used to guide and control a horse.)

Buddha: बुद्ध "The enlightened." Usually refers to Siddhartha Gautama (ca 624–544 BCE), a prince born of a Saivite Hindu tribe that lived in eastern India on the Nepalese border. He renounced the world and became a monk. After his enlightenment he preached the doctrines upon which followers later founded Buddhism.

Calamitous: Disastrous; causing wretchedness and misery.

calamity: Disaster or terrible misfortune.

campaign: An operation or series of operations energetically pursued to accomplish a purpose.

candle: A quantity of wax or other flammable solid, usually cylindrical in shape, which contains a wick; used as a source of light. —**hold a candle:** To compare; to even approach in worthiness or quality. (This expression is used in the negative sense: "This doesn't hold a candle to that.")

Canterbury Tales: See: *Chaucer.*

carcass: Dead body, or empty, lifeless form.

caress: A gentle touch or gesture of fondness, tenderness, or love.

caste: A hierarchical system, called varna dharma (or jati dharma), established in India in ancient times, which determined the privileges, status, rights and duties of the many occupational groups, wherein status is determined by heredity. There are four main classes (varnas)—brahmin, kshatriya, vaishya and shudra—and innumerable castes, called jati.

Caucasian: One of the five races of man. See: *race.*

Caucasoid: Caucasian.

CE: Abbreviation for "common era." Equivalent to the abbreviation AD (*anno Domini,* "in the Lord's [i.e. Christ's] year"). Following a date, it indicates that the year in question comes after the year one in the Western, or Gregorian (originally Christian) calender. E.g., 300 CE is 300 years after the (inexactly calculated) birth of Jesus of Nazareth. Cf: BCE.

celestials: Divine inner-world beings; gods or *devas.*

censure: To blame, find fault with, criticize.

CEO: Chief Executive Officer of a corporation or firm.

chaff: Threshed or winnowed husks of grain. That which is worthless.

chastity: Remaining celibate or faithful to ones spouse, including being virtuous and modest.

Chaucer: Noted English poet, ca 1340(?)-1400 CE; author of *Canterbury Tales*.

cherish: To hold precious; to value highly.

chivalry: The demonstration of noble qualities such as courage, honor or readiness to help.

Chola: Great South Indian dynasty of kings, lasting from 846 CE until 1130 CE.

Christian era: The period beginning with the birth of Jesus Christ. Abbreviated "CE."

civility: Politeness; courtesy.

civilized: Advanced in personal and social refinements; cultured.

classic: A literary work, widely acknowledged as of the highest quality.

classical: Traditional and formal; in conformance with traditional standards of excellence.

cleave: To cling, be united or strongly attached, be faithful.

CNN: Cable News Network, referring to a popular television news channel.

code: A system of accepted behavior, rules, etc. Also, a secret method of communication in which symbols, words, etc. are given other than their usual meanings.

cogent: Convincing, powerful, compelling.

collyrium: A medicated preparation for the eyes.

comic: Amusing, ludicrous, laughable.

commend: To praise or approve. Recommend.

commit: To perpetrate. **—to commit to memory:** To memorize. **—to commit oneself to:** To pledge or bind oneself to a course of action.

compose: To put together; to form by assembling parts. Also, to write an original work. **—to compose oneself:** To quiet the mind and put one's thoughts & emotions in order.

comprehension: Understanding, or the ability to understand.

conceit: Vanity; an overly flattering self-image.

confer: To give, impart or bestow.

confinement: Imprisonment, seclusion; restraint.

confusion: A state of disorder. Also, perplexity, or difficulty in ordering one's thoughts or emotions.

congenial: Compatible, agreeable.

conscience: The inner sense of right and wrong, sometimes called "the knowing voice of the soul."

consequence: A result; also, importance. **—consequent:** Resulting. **—consequently:** As a result.

contain: To hold within. Also, to comprise.

consign: To hand over or assign to an undesirable place.

constituent: Serving as part of a whole; component.

contemporary: Modern; also, existing at the same time period as.

contemptible: Worthless; despicable, deserving scorn.

contention: Strife, argument, quarreling. Asserted belief.

contentious: Antagonistic, argumentative.

continuum: A continuous extent, succession, or whole, no part of which can be distinguished from neighboring parts except by arbitrary division.

contrive: To devise, plan, scheme or plot.

corporal punishment: Physical punishment, as in spanking, inflicted on a child by an adult in authority.

corporate: Having to do with large businesses.

corporate ladder: The hierarchical order of position, title, or rank, as in a large corporation. "To work one's way up the corporate ladder."

corrupt: Morally unsound. Given to involvement with bribery. Also, to cause to become corrupt.

council: A group of people chosen as an administrative or advisory assembly.

countenance: Facial expression, appearance.

counterpart: Someone or something which corresponds to another.

counterweight: Something that is equal in weight to something else, used to provide a counterbalancing action.

couplet: A verse of two lines.

covetousness: Envy; desiring or attempting to get that which others possess.

coyness: A pretended shyness, with the intention of appearing more alluring.

cradle: Environment in which earliest growth or development is made. Originally a baby's small bed.

crafty: Deceitful, fraudulent, sly.

crave: To desire intensely.

cremate: To dispose of a dead body by burning to ashes, thus releasing the soul from attachment to the physical plane.

crooked: Dishonest, deceitful; not straightforward.

crucial: Of supreme importance; decisive; critical.

cumbersome: Difficult to deal with; awkward.

curtail: To cut short, abbreviate; to lessen.

amnation: To condemn as harmful, illegal, or immoral.

damsel: A young unmarried woman.

dawning: A beginning.

dearth: A scarcity, deficiency or lack.

debilitate: To weaken or enfeeble.

decency: Thoughtfulness, courtesy, propriety, seemliness and consideration for others.

deforestation: To cut down and clear away the trees or forests from significant water-shed regions.

deft: Skillfull, sure, precise.

defy: To resist; to refuse to obey.

deliberate: Premeditated; carefully planned beforehand. Slow and careful. Also, to think carefully before acting or deciding.

deliberateness: Calm, careful consideration; caution.

delineate: To mark or trace out the boundaries of a thing, concept, etc.

delineation: A representation or depiction.

deluged: Flooded, overwhelmed, inundated.

depict: To portray or describe.

depraved: Corrupt; morally bad.

deprivation: The loss of something which one has considered important, perhaps something as basic as adequate food, clothing or shelter.

deprived: Dispossessed; having taken something away from; having kept from possessing or enjoying; denied.

desert: To abandon or forsake. Also, a region of little or no rainfall, usually sandy and largely devoid of life.

desertion: The forsaking or leaving of one's military duties or post without permission; especially, running away from the army with no intention of returning.

deserve: To merit or be worthy of; to have earned a particular bit of karma, either pleasant or unpleasant.

desist: To cease, discontinue or permanently abstain from.

destiny: The seemingly inevitable or predetermined course of events. See: *karma.*

destitute: Devoid of; lacking.

destitution: Poverty of the lowest degree.

detached: Impartial, aloof; not emotionally involved.

deva: द्व "Shining one." A Second World being inhabiting the higher astral plane in a subtle, nonphysical body. See: *guardian deva.*

device: A tool or implement. Also, a plan or scheme.

devise: To plan, scheme or contrive.

devoid: Totally without; empty.

Dhammapada: धम्मपद The holy book of Buddhism.

dharma: धर्म From *dhri,* "to sustain; carry, hold." Hence *dharma* is "that which contains or upholds the cosmos." *Dharma* is a complex and all-inclusive term with many meanings, including: divine law, law of being, way of righteousness, religion, duty, responsibility, virtue, justice, goodness and truth. Essentially, *dharma* is the orderly fulfillment of an inherent nature or destiny. Relating to the soul, it is the mode of conduct most conducive to spiritual advancement, the right and righteous path.

diaspora: Any religious group living as a minority among people of the prevailing religion.

dictate: To decree, "from the position of strength;" to command or order with authority.

diligent: Painstaking, steady in effort, marked by perseverance.

diminish: To make or become smaller. To degrade.

dire: Dreadful, dismal, disastrous.

discern: To perceive; distinguish subtle differences.

discernment: The ability to distinguish, discriminate and make balanced judgments.

discourteous: Uncivil, rude.

disparage: To discredit, slight or belittle.

dissension: Disharmony, discord, quarreling or strife.

dissertation: An elaborate scholarly treatise.

distinction: Superior quality, and/or the resulting special recognition.

distinctiveness: Individuality; difference from anything or anyone else.

divination: Act or practice of predicting the future or surmising the best course of action.

divisive: Causing disagreements, divisions.

divulge: To make public, reveal or disclose information previously kept private or secret.

dogmatic: Asserting opinions or doctrines in a positive, possibly arrogant manner; unwillingness to consider any differing evidence, argument, ideas, or insights.

doom: A decision or judgment, especially an official condemnation to a severe penalty.

Doordarshan: A socio-cultural television media program in India.

double-dealing: Deceitful.

downtrodden: Oppressed or subjugated. A state of negative mindedness, where one sees the world around him and his place in it in disarray.

Dravidian: The term used in this text to name the monastic communities of the Dvapara and Kali Yugas. In modern times it refers to the various Caucasoid peoples of southern India and northern Sri Lanka.

dried soil: Soil that has been plowed into friable form, loose, open and well-drained, free of moisture.

dumfounded: Made speechless with astonishment.

dynamic: Vigorous, energetic, active.

echo: A repetition.

eclipse: To outshine, surpass.

ecology: The science of the relationships between organisms and their environments. Also called bionomics.

ecumenical: Universal. —ecumenism: the principles or practices of promoting cooperation and better understanding among differing faiths.

edition: A changed, or revised reissue of a book. Loosely, any reprinting.

efface: To erase.

effeminate: Displaying feminine qualities or behavior such as weakness or undue delicacy; unmanly.

eight infinite powers: Eight attributes of Siva: being self-dependent; being immaculate in body; having intuitive wisdom; being omniscient; being free by nature from all dross or other impurities that fetter souls; being of boundless grace; being omnipotent; and being in enjoyment of boundless bliss.

elaborate: Very detailed and complicated; created with great care, diligence, and attention to detail.

eloquence: Fluency, expressiveness, beauty, and persuasiveness (even compelling) of speech.

elucidate: Explain, clarify or make clear.

embody: To incarnate or give form to.

eminent: High; above others in stature, rank or achievement. Renowned or distinguished; prominent, conspicuous. Not to be confused with: 1) imminent, about to happen; 2) emanate, to issue from; 3) immanent, inherent or indwelling.

emissary: "Sent one." An agent (not necessarily secret) sent on a task or to obtain information.

enchant: To charm, fascinate, or entrance.

encircle: To surround on all sides.

endeavor: A serious attempt. To attempt seriously.

endure: To bear or undergo.

engender: To bring about, or to birth; cause, create or produce.

engulf: To swallow up and submerge.

enjoin: To urge or command.

enliven: To give vitality to.

enmity: Hostility or antagonism.

ensnared: Caught, entangled, trapped.

ensue: To come after, as a result or consequence.

envious: To feel discontented because of others' possessions or advantages.

envoy: A messenger or diplomatic agent.

ephemeral: Evanescent, transitory, fleeting.

epigrammatic: Concise and witty. Literally "inscribed." From such verses often inscribed in stone or metal.

equable: Serene, tranquil, steady.

era: A long period of time, distinguished by particular events or trends. Also a fixed point from which a time-reckoning begins, e.g. Vikramaditya era, Christian era, Muslim era (Hijrah), etc.

erudite: Learned; well researched; scholarly.

erudition: Scholarship; learning obtained through study.

esoteric: Secret, hidden, hard to understand. Teaching intended for a chosen few, as an inner group of initiates. Abstruse or private.

espionage: As used here, information obtained by spying. See: *spy*.

espy: To spy. See: *spy*.

estate: A station in life or possessed valuable property.

estrange: To alienate; turn from a friendly attitude to one of indifference or hostility.

etch: To engrave.

ethical: In conformance with the accepted standards of virtuous conduct; righteous; dharmic.

exalt: To promote or elevate in status; to praise.

execute: To fulfill, administer, or bring into completion; also, to put to death.

exemplar: One regarded as worthy of imitation; a model. An ideal pattern to be followed by others. —**exemplary:** Worthy of being held up as an example; praiseworthy. An ideal that serves as a pattern; an archetype.

exhilaration: A very high, intense, joyful energy. Elation

expend: To use up. Speed up.

expound: To explain, put forth.

expunge: To erase or obliterate; to destroy all trace of.

extol: To praise highly; exalt, as in to extol the virtues of *sadhana* and *seva*.

Fatalism: The doctrine that all events are predetermined by fate and are therefore unalterable.

fate: The supposed force, principle, or power that predetermines events.

fathom: To measure the extent of; to comprehend fully.

faultlessness: The state of not being at fault or to blame for something.

Feet: Here, refers to the holy feet of God. The feet of God are considered especially precious as the source of man's liberation.

feign: To pretend or simulate.

ferret: To investigate and bring out with great diligence and thoroughness; search, find.

fervor: Intense, emotional enthusiasm; zeal.

fetter: Something that serves to restrict; a restraint.

feudal kingdom: Of or relating to a kingdom whose lands are held in fee or to the holding of such lands.

fickle: Variable, changeable, inconstant; capricious.

fierce: As used here, angrily or violently threatening.

five elements: Earth, air, fire, water and ether *(akasha)*, which make up the physical body as well as the rest of the physical universe.

fledgling: A young bird which has grown enough feathers to learn to fly.

fluctuate: To vacillate or vary (in degree, intensity, quality, etc.).

foible: A minor weakness or character flaw.

folded: Hands pressed together, as in the Hindu manner of greeting known as *anjali mudra* or *namaskaram*.

foolhardiness: Rashness, recklessness.

forebode: To augur, portend, foreshadow, usually an undesirable outcome.

foreordain: To determine or appoint beforehand; predestine.

formless: Philosophically, *atattva*, beyond the realm of form or substance. Used in attempting to describe the wondersome, indescribable Absolute, which is "timeless, formless and spaceless." See: Siva.

foundational knowledge: The basis on which a knowledge stands, is founded, or is supported.

fraternity: Brotherhood, company, fellowship, association.

fraud: Deceit; treachery; cheating.

frugal: Thrifty; taking care not to be wasteful or unnecessarily lavish.

furrow: To cut narrow, shallow grooves side by side in the earth, often with a plow, piling the dirt into ridges between these furrows.

andhi: Mohandas Karamchand Gandhi (1869-1948), the Hindu nationalist leader whose strategy of nonviolent resistance won India's freedom from British colonial rule. Often honored as Mahatma ("great soul") Gandhi.

Ganesha: गणेश "Lord of Categories." (From *gan*, "to count or reckon," and *Isha*, "lord.") Or: "Lord of attendants (*gana*)," synonymous with Ganapati. Ganesha is a Mahadeva, the beloved elephant-faced Deity honored by Hindus of every sect. He is the Lord of Obstacles (Vighneshvara), revered for His great wisdom and invoked first before any undertaking, for He knows all intricacies of each soul's *karma* and the perfect path of *dharma* that makes action successful. See: *Mahadeva.*

garland: A wreath or festoon, especially one of plaited flowers or leaves, worn on the body or draped as a decoration.

garner: To amass; acquire, as in to gather and store in or as if in a granary.

gender: Sexual identity, especially in relation to society or culture.

genesis: Origin, source, cause.

glade: An open space in a forest. An everglade.

glutton: One who habitually and greedily eats excessive amounts of food.

God: Supernal being. Either the Supreme God Siva or one of the Mahadevas, great souls, who are among His creation. See: *Gods, Mahadeva, Siva.*

God Primordial: God, Who is not derived from another and Who existed first as the Source of all.

Gods: Mahadevas, "great beings of light." Extremely advanced beings existing in their self-effulgent soul bodies in the causal plane. The meaning of Gods is best seen in the phrase, "God and the Gods," referring to the Supreme God—Siva—and the Mahadevas who are His creation. See: *Mahadeva.*

gorge: To eat greedily; to glut.

grievous: Causing suffering; hard to bear.

guardian *deva:* At the birth of a child, *devas* of the inner worlds are assigned to guard and protect him throughout his life. See: *deva.*

guru mahasannidhanam: गुरु महासन्निधानम् Spiritual head of a traditional aadheenam.

Guru Purnima: गुरु पूर्निमा Occurring on the full moon of July, Guru Purnima is for devotees a day of rededication to all that the guru represents. It is occasioned by *padapuja*—ceremonial worship of the guru's sandals, which represent his holy feet.

guru: "Weighty one," indicating a being of great knowledge or skill. A term used to describe a teacher or guide in any subject, such as music, dance, sculpture, but especially religion.

allmark: An indicator or evidence of high quality or authenticity. Originally a mark on silver and gold articles stamped at Goldsmiths' Hall in London as a symbol of approved standards.

harbor: To house or shelter; to hold and protect.

harlot: A prostitute. A mercenary, promiscuous and seductive woman.

heir: One who inherits, or is expected to inherit, property from another.

hell: *Naraka.* An unhappy, mentally and emotionally congested, distressful area of consciousness. Hell is a state of mind that can be experienced on the physical plane or in the sub-astral plane *(Naraka)* after death of the physical body. It is accompanied by the tormented emotions of hatred, remorse, resentment, fear, jealousy and self-condemnation. However, in the Hindu view, the hellish experience is not permanent, but a temporary condition of one's own making.

henpeck: To dominate or harass (one's husband) with persistent nagging.

herald: To proclaim, announce.

heritage: A tradition passed down from preceding generations as an inheritance.

heron: A large bird which wades stealthily through shallow water, then stands motionless until its prey swims or crawls within striking distance.

Hinduism *(Hindu Dharma):* हिन्दुधर्म India's indigenous religious and cultural system, followed today by nearly one billion adherents, mostly in India, but with large populations in many other countries. Also called Sanatana Dharma, "eternal religion" and Vaidika Dharma, "religion of the *Vedas*." Hinduism is the world's most ancient religion and encompasses a broad spectrum of philosophies ranging from pluralistic theism to absolute monism. It is a family of myriad faiths with four primary denominations: Saivism, Vaishnavism, Shaktism and Smartism. These four hold such divergent beliefs that each is a complete and independent religion. Yet, they share a vast heritage of culture and belief— karma, dharma, reincarnation, all-pervasive Divinity, temple worship, sacraments, manifold Deities, the *guru-shishya* tradition and a reliance on the *Vedas* as scriptural authority.

hinge: A pivotal device, used for attaching a door to a wall, etc.

hoard: To hide; store away; keep in reserve.

homage: Special honor or respect shown or expressed publicly.

hospitality: Cordial and generous reception of or disposition toward guests.

householder: *Grihastha.* Family man or woman; pertaining to family life. One who follows the path of family life (as opposed to that of the renunciate). In Hinduism, family life is one of serving, learning and striving within a close-knit community of many relatives, under the guidance of a spiritual guru.

hub: Center of a wheel. Center of interest, importance or activity.

humility: Awareness of one's shortcomings; modesty.

ice age: Extended period of time when glaciers expand to cover much of the earth's surface.

icon: An image; a representation. A simile or symbol.

imbed: To set firmly in place.

immanent: Indwelling; inherent and operating within. Relating to God, the term immanent means present in all things and throughout the universe, not aloof or distant. Not to be confused with imminent (about to happen), emanate (to issue from), or eminent (high in rank).

immense: Vast, immeasurable.

immutable: Unchangeable.

impartiality: Freedom from bias or favoritism; the condition of being unprejudiced and equitable.

impeccable: Faultless; flawless; without error.

impel: To urge to action through moral pressure.

imperceptible: Impossible or difficult to perceive by the mind or senses.

imperturbable: Calm, serene, mentally unshakable; not subject to being disturbed or disconcerted.

implementation: The putting into effect or carrying out of a plan.

imply: To indicate indirectly; to hint or suggest.

impose: To inflict upon, uninvited and unrightfully.

impoverished: Very poor; deprived of strength.

inane: Empty; void of meaning; foolish.

incessant: Unceasing; continuing without pause or interruption.

incinerate: To burn to ashes.

incomparable: Unequaled, without a match, beyond comparison.

inconceivable: That cannot be imagined or believed.

inconsequential: Of no consequence; trivial; insignificant.

indifference: Lack of concern, apathy; unaffectedness.

indispensable: Essential; absolutely necessary.

indolence: Habitual idleness; laziness.

indolent: Disinclined to exert oneself; habitually lazy.

Indra: इन्द्र Ruler. Vedic God of rain and thunder, warrior king of the *devas*.

indulgence: Leniency or special favors.

indulgent: Lenient; excessively permissive; maintaining little or no restraint or control.

inescapably: Unavoidably; inevitably.

infatuation: Folly; irrational attraction or passion.

infidel: An unbeliever with respect to a particular religion, especially Christianity or Islam.

infiltrate: To pass into, through openings or weak spots; often with hostile intent.

Infinity: God as the infinite, endless, unlimited with respect to space and time.

inflammatory: Characterized by or tending to rouse anger or violence.

inflamed: Aroused with passion, violence or anger.

influence: To modify; to have an effect on; also, the ability to affect the thoughts or actions of others.

information spy: One who observes and reports to interested parties the activities of others.

iniquity: Lack of righteousness or virtue.

initiation: A bringing into, or admitting as a member. In Hinduism, initiation from a qualified preceptor is considered invaluable for spiritual progress.

innate: Inborn, inherent.

inner worlds: The second and third worlds, in the Hindu view of the cosmos. See: *three worlds.*

instinctive: "Natural or innate." From the Latin *instinctus*, "impelling, instigating." The drives and impulses that rule the animal world and the physical and lower astral aspects of humans—for example, self-preservation, procreation, hunger, and the emotions of greed, hatred, anger, fear, lust and jealousy.

intention: A purpose or plan.

interactions: Reciprocal actions; dealings.

interminable: Endless or seemingly endless.

Internet: Worldwide network of computers which facilitates the efficient transmission and exchange of information among people all over the world. Conceived in 1969 as ARPANET, a U.S. Department of Defense research test-bed, the Internet has grown rapidly from 1994 to the present as the benefits of hypertext (the concept that made the World Wide Web possible) and the multimedia capabilities of the technology became popular among mainstream culture. A globally-extended Internet is quickly becoming what has been predicted to be the key unifying communications technology of the next century.

intrepidity: Fearlessness.

intrinsic: Inward; essential; inherent. Belonging to the real nature of a being or thing.

intuition (to **intuit**): Direct understanding or cognition, which bypasses the process of reason but does not contradict reason.

intuitive: Having to do with intuition.

invigorating: To impart vigor, strength, or vitality to; animate.

irreparable: Damaged, and unable to be restored to its former state.

Islamic era: The beginnings of the Nation of Islam 1,400 years ago, founded by

Mohammed.

Itihasa: इतिहास "So it was." Epic history, particularly the *Ramayana* and *Mahabharata* (of which the famed *Bhagavad Gita* is a part).

Jackal: A nocturnal wild dog native to Asia and northern Africa which hunts in packs.

Jagadacharya: जगदाचार्य "World teacher." In 1986 the World Religious Parliament of New Delhi named five world leaders who were most active in spreading Sanatana Dharma outside India.

Jain: जैन Of or having to do with Jainism; a member of that religion.

Jainism: A religion founded about 2,500 years ago in India. Its supreme ideal is *ahimsa,* nonviolence, stressing equal kindness and reverence for all life.

japa: जप "Recitation." Practice of concentrated repeating of a mantra, often while counting the repetitions on a *mala* or strand of beads. It may be done silently or aloud. Sometimes known as mantra yoga. See: *mala.*

jequirity: The poisonous seed of the Indian licorice plant (Abrus precatorius), so striking in appearance that it is used for beads.

Jesus: The most famous person of this name is Jesus of Nazareth, a Jewish carpenter and itinerant religious teacher, whose followers later founded the Christian religion. They consider him an incarnation of the Supreme God (Son of God), and revere him as Jesus Christ, the surname translating the Hebrew Messiah.

journeyman: One who has fully served an apprenticeship in a trade or craft and is a qualified worker in another's employ.

jubilant: Joyful, exultant.

jyotisha shastri: ज्योतिषशास्त्री "Astrologer." A person well versed in the science of *jyotisha.*

jyotisha: ज्योतिष From *jyoti,* "light." "The science of the lights (or stars)." Hindu astrology, the knowledge and practice of analyzing events and circumstances, delineating character and determining auspicious moments, according to the positions and movements of heavenly bodies. In calculating horoscopes, *jyotisha* uses the sidereal (fixed-star) system, whereas Western astrology uses the tropical (fixed-date) method.

Kadavul: கடவுள் "Beyond and within." An ancient Tamil name for Lord Siva meaning, "He who is both immanent and transcendent, within and beyond."

Kailasa Parampara: कैलासपरंपरा A spiritual lineage of 162 siddhas, a major stream of the Nandinatha Sampradaya, proponents of the ancient philosophy of monistic Saiva Siddhanta.

kama: Pleasure, love, desire. Cultural, intellectual and sexual fulfillment.

karma: The law of action and reaction, cause and effect, by which our thoughts, words and deeds create our future. One's karma must be in a state of quiescent balance, or fulfillment, in order for liberation to be attained. It is this state of resolution that all Hindus seek through making amends and settling differences.

Kauai Aadheenam: Monastery-temple complex founded by Sivaya Subramuniyaswami in 1970; international headquarters of Saiva Siddhanta Church.

keen: Sharp; vivid; strong; eager, enthusiastic.

Koran: The Islamic religion's sacred book, God's word transmitted through the angel Gabriel to Mohammed, the prophet of Islam. Its official version appeared around 650, 18 years after Mohammed's death. See: *Mohammed.*

Kumbha Mela: A periodic gathering of a large number of Hindu devotees at the river Ganga, celebrating the tradition that drops of *amrita*, the divine nectar of immortality, fell at four holy places in India: Haridwar, Allahabad, Nasik and Ujjain.

ady-in-waiting: A close female attendant to a lady.

Lakshmi: लक्ष्मी "Mark or sign," often of success or prosperity. Shakti, the Universal Mother, as Goddess of wealth. The mythological consort of Vishnu, usually depicted on a lotus flower. Prayers are offered to Lakshmi for wealth, beauty and peace.

lament: A feeling or an expression of grief; a lamentation.

lamp black: The black, carbonized substance which forms on a burning lamp.

lance: A thrusting weapon with a long shaft; a spear.

languid: Adjective of *languor.* See: *languor.*

languor: Lack of vigor or vitality; listlessness; lethargy; lassitude.

lattice: An open, net-like structure, usually made of thin boards.

lewd: Lustful, licentious, immodest, shameless; preoccupied with sex and sexual desire.

liberation: Moksha, release from the bonds of *pasam*, after which the soul is liberated from *samsara* (the round of births and deaths). In Saiva Siddhanta, *pasam* is the three-fold bondage of *anava, karma* and *maya*, which limit and confine the soul to the reincarnational cycle so that it may evolve. Moksha is freedom from the fettering power of these bonds, which do not cease to exist, but no longer have the power to fetter or bind the soul. See: *anava, karma, maya, pasam.*

licentious: Morally unrestrained, especially in sexual behavior. Also, tending to arouse sexual impulses.

linchpin: The small pin which secures a wheel to its axle. A central cohesive element or functionality.

liquor: Strong alcoholic drink produced by distillation, such as whisky or rum.

localized: Existing within a specific area.

lofty: Very high, exalted, noble.

loom: A simple machine on which cloth is woven.

lotus: A flowering aquatic plant, *Nelumbo nucifera*, and especially its flower, which is used as a symbol of spiritual development and the *chakras*. Because it grows out of mud and rises to perfect purity and glory, it is an apt representation of spiritual unfoldment.

love-sickness: An incapacitating distraction, or pining, caused by overwhelming emotions of love, yearning, etc.

lunatic: An insane person. Originally a lunatic's condition was supposed to be intensified with the phases of the moon (Latin *luna*).

luster: A bright, glossy, or shining quality.

lustful: Filled with desire, usually sexual.

Magnificent: Splendid, imposing, glorious.

Mahabharata: महाभरत "Great Epic of India." The world's longest epic poem. It revolves around the conflict between two kingdoms, the Pandavas and Kauravas, and their great battle of Kurukshetra near modern Delhi in approximately 1424 BCE. Woven through the plot are countless discourses on philosophy, religion, astronomy, cosmology, polity, economics and many stories illustrative of simple truths and ethical principles. The *Bhagavad Gita* is one section of the work. The *Mahabharata* is revered as scripture by Vaishnavites and Smartas. See: *Bhagavad Gita, Itihasa.*

Mahadeva: महादेव "Great shining one; God." Referring either to God Siva or any of the highly evolved beings who live in the Sivaloka in their natural, effulgent soul bodies. God Siva in His perfection as Primal Soul is one of the Mahadevas, yet He is unique and incomparable in that He alone is uncreated, the Father-Mother and Destiny of all other Mahadevas. He is called Parameshvara, "Supreme God." He is the Primal Soul, whereas the other Gods are individual souls.

mahatma: Great soul. Also used as a title of honor.

mala: माला "Garland." A strand of beads for holy recitation, *japa*, usually made of *rudraksha, tulasi,* sandalwood or crystal. See: *japa.*

malady: Sickness, affliction.

malicious: Full of enmity; spiteful, malevolent.

manifest: To come (or coming) into existence.

marital: Of or relating to marriage.

marvel: A wonderful, perhaps even miraculous, thing.

marvelous: Strange and wonderful; extraordinary.

maya: माया "Artfulness," "illusion," "phantom" or "mirific energy." The substance emanated from Siva through which the world of form is manifested. Hence all creation is also termed *maya.* It is the cosmic creative force, the principle of manifestation, ever in the process of creation, preservation and dissolution.

meagerly: Deficient in quantity, fullness or extent; scanty. Deficient in richness, fertility or vigor; feeble.

meditate: To sustain the state of concentration, achieving a quiet, alert, powerfully concentrated state wherein new knowledge and insights are awakened from within as awareness focuses one-pointedly on an object or specific line of thought. **—meditation:** The result of successful concentration; uninterrupted thought on a subject, leading to intuitive discovery.

medium: A means, as of communication. The plural, **media,** refers to the public communication industry as a whole, including books, magazines, newspapers, television, etc.

mercenary: Performing services for monetary payment.

merit: A worthy quality; also, to be worthy of.

messenger: One who carries a message.

migrate: To move from one place to another.

millennium: A period of 1,000 years. **—millennia:** Plural of millennium.

minister: An official charged with a specific function on behalf of a political authority. In religious context, a clergyman authorized to conduct worship and serve the spiritual needs of the congregation.

minute: Tiny, precise.

miraculous: Marvelous, and inexplicable.

mire: An area of wet, soggy, muddy ground; a bog. Deep, slimy soil or mud to describe a disadvantageous or difficult condition or situation.

miser: Someone who avariciously gathers and hoards wealth, usually driven by fear of poverty.

miserliness: Greediness, stinginess.

misery: A great unhappiness, calamity, pain or ache.

missionary: One who is engaged in spreading the teachings of his religion.

mock: To treat scornfully or contemptuously; deride.

Mohammed: Founder of the Islam religion. See: *Islam.*

moksha: See: *liberation.*

monarch: The ruler of a monarchy: a king, queen, or emperor.

monk: A celibate man wholly dedicated to religious life; a monastic. See: *sannyasa, swami.*

morsel: A small, bite-sized portion of food.

motivate: To impel or give impetus to.

mountainous: Like a mountain, especially in size or height. Full of mountains.

multitude: A great number; a crowd or swarm.

murky: Dark, devoid of light, gloomy, dismal.

Muslim: A follower of Islam. See: *Islam.*

mystic: One who understands religious mysteries or occult rites and practices. Inspiring a sense of mystery and wonder.

andinatha Sampradaya: नन्दिनाथसंप्रदाय See: *Natha Sampradaya.*

Nataraja: नटराज "King of Dance," or "King of Dancers." God as the Cosmic Dancer. Perhaps Hinduism's richest and most eloquent symbol,

Nataraja represents Siva, the Primal Soul, Parameshvara, as the power, energy and life of all that exists.

Narakaloka: See: *Hell.*

Natha Sampradaya: नाथसंप्रदाय "Traditional doctrine of the masters." Sampradaya means a living stream of tradition or theology. Natha Sampradaya, the oldest of Saivite *sampradayas* existing today, consists of two major streams: the Nandinatha and the Adinatha.

nation: A people of a country as a political entity.

nature: The character, disposition, or essence of a thing. Also, the physical universe, especially its laws and life processes.

negligence: Carelessness, neglectfulness; habitual failure to do what needs to be done.

Newsweek: A popular weekly news magazine published in the United States.

nobility: The quality of having noble characteristics.

nobleman: A person of heredity rank or title, such as the English peer, duke, earl, etc.

noninvolvement: Detachment; state of being uninvolved or unentangled.

nonviolence: See: *ahimsa.*

novice: A person new to a field or activity; a beginner.

numerology: The study of the hidden meanings of numbers and how they influence human life.

nymph: A super-human or astral seductress.

Objective: A target, goal or anything sought for or aimed at.

obliterate: To wipe out; to destroy all trace of.

oblivious: Unmindful, unaware; forgetful.

obscure: Not clearly understood or explained; dark, vague.

oceanic: Of or pertaining to the ocean; huge.

odd: Unusual; strange.

odious: Hateful; abhorrent.

office: A position which carries authority, or the functions or duties of such a position.

official: Authorized or authoritative agent.

ogre: A man-eating giant of folklore.

ogress: A female ogre.

olai: ஓலை One of various species of palm, the long-lasting leaves of which have been used in India and Sri Lanka since ancient times for recording scriptures and other literature, by scratching the words into the leaf's surface.

olden: Long-ago.

operative: A detective or spy. See: *spy.*

opposition: Anyone who tries to obstruct one's plans or interests; also, the obstacles or challenges put forth as part of such effort.

oppression: The imposition of excessive taxes or other burdens; harsh government.

opulent: Profuse, abundant, very rich.

oral: Spoken, rather than written.

ostensibly: Claimed or believed by some to be.

outflank: To move alongside or beyond (an enemy's troops) in order to gain a more advantageous position.

outmoded: Obsolete.

outstretch: To extend, to stretch out, as one's arms or a large cloth.

overflow: To spread past the edges or beyond the limits.

agan: One who is not a Christian, Muslim or Jew; a heathen. Paganism is a spiritual way of life which has its roots in the ancient nature religions of the world. It is principally identified with the old religions of Europe and regions to the east, such as in parts of Ukraine. Pagans celebrate the sanctity of nature, recognize the divine in all things and are accepting and tolerant of all religious expression. In the broad sense, Hindus are also Pagans.

pal: A friend.

palanquin: A covered couch carried by poles on the shoulders of two or more men.

pandit: पण्डित A Hindu religious scholar or theologian, a man well versed in philosophy, liturgy, religious law and sacred science.

Pandya: Great South Indian kingdom, 300 BCE-1700 CE.

panegyric: High praise.

pang: A sharp pain; a spasm of distress; agony.

parallel: To correspond closely alongside, as in purpose or essential parts.

parentheses: Curved written symbols (such as those containing this example) which enclose a sentence or idea which is additional, and tangential or explanatory to, a sentence or paragraph which is already complete without it.

parliamentarian: One who is expert in parliamentary procedures, rules, or debate.

particular: Specific. —**particularly:** Especially.

Parvati: पार्वती "Mountain's daughter." One of many names for the Universal Mother. Prayers are offered to Her for strength, health and eradication of impurities. Mythologically, Parvati is wedded to Siva.

pasam: पाश or பாசம் "Tether; noose." The whole of existence, manifest and unmanifest. That which binds or limits the soul and keeps it (for a time) from manifesting its full potential. *Pasam* refers to the soul's three-fold bondage of *anava, karma* and *maya.* See: *anava, karma, maya, mala, liberation, pasu, Pati-pasu-pasam.*

passion: Any extreme, overpowering emotion, including strong sexual desire, or lust; also, an overwhelming drive to do something.

pasu: पशु or பசு "Cow, cattle, kine; fettered individual." Refers to animals or beasts, including man. In philosophy, the soul. See: *pasam, Pati-pasu-pasam.*

Patanjali: पतञ्जलि A Saivite Natha *siddha* (ca 200 BCE) who codified the ancient yoga philosophy which outlines the path to enlightenment through purification, control and transcendence of the mind. See: *Yoga Sutras.*

Pati: पति or பதி "Master; lord; owner." An appellation of God Siva indicating His commanding relationship with souls as caring ruler and helpful guide. See: *Pati-pasu-pasam, Siva.*

Pati-pasu-pasam: पति पशु पाश or பதி பசு பாசம் Literally: "master, cow and tether." These are the three primary elements of Saiva Siddhanta philosophy: God, soul and world—Divinity, man and cosmos—seen as a mystically and intricately interrelated unity. *Pati* is God, envisioned as a cowherd. *Pasu* is the soul, envisioned as a cow. *Pasam* is the all-important force or fetter by which God brings souls along the path to Truth.

peerless: Without equal; matchless.

penance: *Prayashchitta.* Atonement, expiation. An act of devotion *(bhakti)*, austerity *(tapas)* or discipline *(sukritya)* undertaken to soften or nullify the anticipated reaction to a past action.

penitents: Those who repent their misdeeds, especially those who perform penance to atone for their wrongful actions.

perceive: To understand or comprehend. To become aware of directly through any of the senses, especially sight or hearing, and the third eye, a*jna chakra.*

perception: Awareness (either sensory or intuitive).

perilous: Dangerous; hazardous.

perpetuate: To preserve; to cause to endure.

perplex: To confuse or bewilder.

persistence: Constancy, resoluteness. Continuous effort.

pervade: To permeate or be present throughout.

perverse: Distorted or deviating from dharma; acting on adharmic priorities.

philanthropist: One who practices charity in a desire to help others. Literally (from Greek) "loving people." **—philanthropy:** The desire to benefit humanity, especially through charitable gifts, etc.

pierced: Stabbed, perforated.

pilgrimage: *Tirthayatra,* one of the five sacred duties *(pancha nitya karmas)* of the Hindu is to journey periodically to one of the innumerable holy spots in India or other countries. Preceded by fasting and continence, it is a time of austerity and purification, when all worldly concerns are set aside and God becomes one's singular focus.

pinnacle: The culminating or highest point; apex.

pious: Having or exhibiting religious reverence; earnestly compliant in the observance of religion; devout.

pity: A feeling of sympathy for the sadness, pain, or troubles of another.

plot: A story line; also, to make harmful or dishonest plans.

plummet: To fall precipitously downward.

ply: To work at; steadily attend to.

ponder: To think carefully and deliberately about; to consider deeply.

Pongal: Tai Pongal, தைப்பொங்கல் A four-day home festival held in the Tamil month of Tai (January-February), celebrating the season's first harvest.

portray: To depict or represent.

posterity: Succeeding generations; offspring; the future.

postulate: To claim or assume as self-evident.

posture: A position of the body.

potentate: One who possesses great power, as a ruler or monarch.

praise: To express high approval of; to laud or extol. Also, laudation, approbation.

prattle: To chatter.

prayashchitta: See: *Penance.*

precede: To come before in time, importance, influence or rank.

predetermined: To determine, decide, or establish in advance. See: *Fatalism, Fate.*

predicate: In grammar, that which is said about the subject of a sentence or clause.

predominate: To be in the majority, or to have dominance over others.

premonition: A feeling that something is about to happen.

presence: The condition of being at that place and time; immediate proximity.

prestige: exalted reputation, distinction, high status.

prevail: To be strong and victorious; overcome all obstacles. To exist widely.

prevalent: Prevailing; commonly occuring, accepted.

primordial: See: *God Primordial.*

principle: An essential truth, law or rule upon which others are based.

privation: The lack of customary necessities and comforts.

prodigious: Extraordinary, enormous; powerful.

proffer: To offer, usually something intangible.

proficient: Having or marked by an advanced degree of ability, as in an art, craft, profession or knowledge. **—proficiency:** The condition of being proficient; skillfulness, expertise.

profuse: "Free flowing." Abundantly generous.

proliferate: To increase in numbers rapidly.

propensity: Inclination, disposition, or tendency.

prophetic: Predicts or foreshadows.

proportionate: Existing in a fixed ratio.

propriety: Adherence to accepted standards of conduct; appropriateness, seemliness, decency.

prose: Any literature or speech which is not poetry; everyday language, unrhymed and unmetered.

prospective: Anticipated, expected.

protocol: Customs of proper etiquette, form and ceremony, especially in relation to religious or political dignitaries.

providence: Care, guardianship and control exercised by God; divine direction.

prowess: Superior ability or accomplishment.

puja: पूजा "Worship, adoration." A Hindu rite of worship performed in the home, temple or shrine. Its inner purpose is to purify the atmosphere around the object worshiped, establish a connection with the inner worlds and invoke the presence of God, Gods or one's guru.

punarjanma: Reincarnation. From *punah,* "again and again," and *janma,* "taking birth."

puppet: One whose behavior is determined by the will of others; like a marionette, a figure having jointed parts animated from above by strings or wires.

purnima: पूर्निमा "Full." Full moon. See: *Guru Purnima.*

uell: To quiet, allay or pacify.
query: A question.
quintessence: The ultimate, pure essence of something; its most pure and complete manifestation.

ace: Technically, each of the five races of man (Caucasoid, Mongoloid, Australoid, Congoid and Capoid) is a *Homo sapiens* subspecies. A subspecies is a branch showing slight but significant differences from another branch living in a different area. More generally: any geographical, national or tribal ethnic group, or to mankind as a whole, as "the human race."

radical: Basic, fundamental. Also, drastic, extreme.

raiments: Garments, clothing, attire.

Rajaraja Chola: राजराजचोळ Greatest of the Chola kings, reigning from 985-1014.

Ramayana: रामायन "Life of Rama." One of India's two grand epics (Itihasa) along with the *Mahabharata.* It is Valmiki's tragic love story of Rama and Sita, whose exemplary lives have helped set high standards of dignity and nobility as an integral part of Hindu dharma.

rancor: Bitter hatred, spite or malice; ill will; enmity.

random: Haphazard; without conscious choice.

range: Extent or scope, indicating the amount of possible variation.

raptly: With absorbed attention and great interest.

rapture: Great joy; ecstasy; bliss.

rasp: A coarse file with sharp points on its surface. To utter in a grating voice. To grate on (nerves or feelings).

ratify: To confirm; to officially approve for implementation.

ratio: The relation of one quantity to another; proportion.

ravage: To violently destroy.

realize: To become cognizant of; to grasp mentally; to comprehend.

reap: To obtain a return or reward as in to harvest (a crop).

recitation: A recital, especially in public. **—recite:** To repeat aloud from memory.

reel: To stagger, attempting to regain one's balance.

refine: To purify. **—refined:** Purified. Also, elegant or subtle.

reflect: To shine back the likeness of; to mirror. Also, to consider carefully.

refrain: To hold oneself back; to forbear; to control the impulse to do something.

refugee: One who flees in search of refuge, as in times of war, political oppression, or religious persecution.

reincarnation: *Punarjanma.* Rebirth of the soul in another body. A rebirth in another form; a new embodiment.

relatively: In relation to something else.

relevant: Meaningful in relation to the current situation or topic; pertinent.

relinquish: To give up or abandon; renounce.

renouncer: See: *Renunciate.*

renown: Fame; excellent reputation deriving from accomplishment. **—renowned:** Famous.

renunciate: One who has renounced all attachment to the world, its pleasures and goals, in his one-pointed striving for liberation; a sannyasin.

replica: A copy.

repose: Rest, calm, tranquility, freedom from worry; peace of mind.

reproach: Blame, accusation; disgrace.

reprove: To rebuke, chide or reprehend; to express disapproval.

request: To ask for; an asking for something; something asked for.

resilient: Having the ability to spring back to its natural form after being subjected to stress; able to quickly recover in vigor, enthusiasm, etc. Elasticity.

resistance: Opposition.

resolutely: Determinedly, firmly, with confidence. **—resoluteness:** Determination, perseverance.

resolve: To explain, clarify; to settle or set to rest; to dissolve.

responsiveness: Quickness to respond or comply.

restrain: To control; hold back.

resurgence: A reviving, resurrection or re-strengthening.

retaliation: Returning a wrong for a wrong received. Vengeance

retribution: Punishment, retaliation.

revelation: A vision or sudden understanding.

revelry: Loud, disorderly merrymaking; boisterousness.

revere: To respect with love and devotion. **—reverence:** A feeling of great love, respect and devotion; veneration.

revolve: To circle around; to be centered around.

rhyme: A uniform rhythm containing repetitive, similar sounds, especially at the end of lines. (A quality of some verse forms).

rishi: ऋषि "Seer." A term for an enlightened being, emphasizing psychic perception and visionary wisdom.

rival: To equal or surpass, as in a competition.

rogue: An unprincipled, deceitful, and unreliable person; a rascal or scoundrel. See: *scoundrel.*

role model: Someone whose behavior others attempt to emulate as their ideal.

sadhana: साधन "Effective means of attainment." Religious or spiritual disciplines, such as *puja,* yoga, meditation, *japa,* fasting and austerity. The effect of *sadhana* is the building of willpower, faith and confidence in oneself and in God, Gods and guru.

sadhu: साधु "Virtuous one; straight, unerring." A holy person dedicated to the search for God.

sage: A person respected for his spiritual wisdom and judgement.

saint: A holy man or woman, devoid of ego, whose devout life reflects his or her inner peace, humility, and purity.

Saiva Siddhanta: शैवसिद्धान्त "Final conclusions of Saivism." The most widespread and influential Saivite school today, predominant especially among the Tamil people in Sri Lanka and South India. It is the formalized theology of the divine revelations contained in the twenty-eight *Saiva Agamas.* Other sacred scriptures include the *Tirumantiram* and the voluminous collection of devotional hymns, the *Tirumurai,* and the masterpiece on ethics and statecraft, the *Tirukural.* See: *Hinduism, Saivism.*

Saivism *(Saiva):* शैव The religion followed by those who worship Siva as supreme God. Oldest of the four sects of Hinduism. See: *Hinduism, Saiva Siddhanta.*

salvation: The realization of our unity with God, followed by liberation from rebirth. See: *liberation, Pati-pasu-pasam.*

Sanatana Dharma: सनातनधर्म "Eternal religion" or "everlasting path." It is a traditional name for the Hindu religion.

sanctify: To make holy; to purify or consecrate.

sannyasa (-in): संन्यास "Renunciation." "Throwing down" or "abandoning." Sannyasa is the repudiation of the *dharma,* including the obligations and duties, of the householder and the assumption of the even more demanding dharma of the renunciate. **—sannyasin:** "Renouncer." One who has taken *sannyasa diksha,* the vows of *sannyasa.* A Hindu monk.

sap: To drain the vital force of; to weaken; to undermine.

satguru: सद्गुरु "True weighty one." A spiritual preceptor of the highest attainment—one who has realized the ultimate Truth, Parasiva, through *nirvikalpa samadhi*—a *jivanmukta* able to lead others securely along the spiritual path. He is always a *sannyasin,* an unmarried renunciate.

savor: To appreciate, enjoy tasting, or relish.

savory: Enticing in taste or smell; deliciously salty, piquant, pungent or spicy.

scepter: The staff and insigne of royal or imperial authority and power held by a spiritual monarch or king.

scoff: To deride, mock or ridicule. An expression of derision or scorn.

scorn: To treat with disdain or contempt.

scoundrel: A mean, base, unscrupulous person; a stranger to dharma.

scourge: Whip, flog severely. Metaphorically suffering, affliction.

scribe: To write. Also, a person who writes things down, especially as dictated by another or copied.

sectarian: Characteristic of a sect. A narrow adherent to the beliefs of a specific sect, especially in the conviction that all other sects are incorrect or incomplete.

Self: Self-God. God Siva's Perfection of Absolute Reality, Parasiva, that which abides at the core of every soul.

self-oblivion: Complete forgetfulness or unmindfulness of problems, priorities, or dharma; mental vacancy, usually produced by alcohol or drugs. See: *stupor.*

self-reflective: Characterized by or given to meditation or contemplation; thoughtful of one's self.

Sermon on the Mount: A teaching of Jesus of Nazareth, part of the Christian Bible. See: *Jesus.*

servitude: The state of involuntary subjection to another; slavery; bondage.

shamelessness: The lack of shame, modesty or decency.

shloka: श्लोक A verse, phrase, proverb or hymn of praise, usually composed in a specified meter. Especially a verse of two lines, each of sixteen syllables.

shrewd: Keen-witted, astute.

shuttle: An instrument that carries a spool of thread in the weaving of cloth.

Sikh: Of or having to do with Sikhism; a member of that religion. —**Sikhism:** A religion founded about 500 years ago in India, in opposition to the caste system and the use of images for worship.

sin: Intentional transgression of divine law. Hinduism does not view sin as a crime against God, but as an act against dharma—moral order—and one's own self. It is thought natural, if unfortunate, that young souls act wrongly, for they are living in ignorance. In Hinduism, there are no such concepts as original, inherent or mortal sin. See: *dharma, anava.*

siren: In Greek and Roman mythology, sirens were a kind of sea nymph whose seductive singing lured sailors to their death.

Siva: शिव The "Auspicious," "Gracious," or "Kindly one." Supreme Being of the Saivite religion. God Siva is All and in all, simultaneously the creator and the creation, both immanent and transcendent. As personal Deity, He is Creator, Preserver and Destroyer. He is a one Being, perhaps best understood in three perfections: Parameshvara (Primal Soul), Parashakti (Pure Consciousness) and Parasiva (Absolute Reality).

Sivaloka: "World of Siva," and of the Gods and highly evolved souls. The causal plane, also called Karanaloka, existing deep within the Antarloka at a higher level of vibration, it is a world of superconsciousness and extremely refined energy. It is the plane of creativity and intuition, the quantum level of the universe, where souls exists in self-effulgent bodies made of actinic particles of light. It is here that God and Gods move and lovingly guide the evolution of all the worlds and shed their ever-flowing grace.

slab: A large flat piece, usually of stone.

sloth: Sluggishness, indolence, idleness, laziness.

slumber: Sleep (both as a noun and as a verb).

smear: To apply with a rubbing or stroking motion.

soap opera: A type of drama, usually broadcast on radio or television, in which the emphasis is mostly on emotional turmoil.

sordid: Low-minded, vile, mean. Morally "dirty."

sorely: Painfully.

soul: The real being of man, as distinguished from body, mind and emotions. The soul—known as atman or *purusha*—is the sum of its two aspects, the form or body of the soul and the essence of the soul (though many texts use the word soul to refer to the essence only). **—essence or nucleus of the soul:** Man's innermost and unchanging being—Pure Consciousness (Parashakti or Satchidananda) and Absolute Reality (Parasiva). This essence was never created, does not change or evolve and is eternally identical with God Siva's perfections of Parashakti and Parasiva.

sovereign: The ruler of a country; the holder of the highest political authority.

sow: To scatter (seed) over the ground for growing.

spaceless: Unbounded by spatial considerations; unlimited; not circumscribed by dimensions.

spark: A small piece of burning matter, especially thrown off by fire. To set afire; to ignite, kindle, or activate.

spiritual: Having to do with the spirit (soul, inner being) of man.

spy: To clandestinely investigate or observe in order to obtain secret information; also, a person employed in spying.

squander: To expend recklessly and extravagantly.

stalwart: Strong, sturdy; brave.

stanza: A group of lines of a verse forming a recurrent pattern.

stature: Extent of development—whether referring to physical height or such aspects as political, scholarly or spiritual achievement.

stoic: Indifferent to emotion or passion. The ideal of Stoic philosophy of ancient Greeks and Romans.

stratum: A section or layer of something. Plural: strata.

strut: A haughty, swaggering walk; to display in order to impress others.

stun: To daze or make unconscious (by a blow). Also, to astonish.

stupor: Dullness of mind or senses, as from alcohol or narcotics; a daze.

stylus: A sharp, hand-held implement used for scratching marks onto leaves or other surfaces.

subconscious: The subconscious mind: the storehouse of past impressions, reactions and desires and the seat of involuntary physiological processes.

subdued: Conquered, overcome; reduced.

subsist: To remain alive.

subtle: Keen, acute, penetrating; also, elusive, delicate, not obvious.

success: Accomplishment of a goal, often the goal of obtaining wealth.

succinct: Brief, concise, and clearly stated.

succumb: To submit to an overpowering force or yield to an overwhelming desire; give up or give in.

sulk: To behave in a resentful, sullen manner, rejecting friendly or courteous overtures. **—the sulks:** Sulky behavior.

sundry: Various; diverse.

superconscious: Having to do with The mind of light, the all-knowing intelligence of the soul. At its deepest level, the superconscious is Parashakti, or Satchidananda, the Divine Mind of God Siva. Shining through the purified subconscious, it brings forth intuition, clarity and insight.

superfluous: Unnecessary, irrelevant.

supplicate: To beseech, implore or beg.

surge: To billow violently, as waves on a stormy sea.

surpass: To excel; to be superior to.

suspend: To hang from something.

sustain: To uphold, maintain or provide for; also, to experience.

swami: स्वामी "Lord; owner." He who knows or is master of himself. A respectful title for a Hindu monk, usually a sannyasin, an initiated, orange-robed renunciate, dedicated wholly to religious life. As a sign of respect, the term swami is sometimes applied more broadly to include nonmonastics dedicated to spiritual work. See: *monk, renunciate, sannyasa.*

sweat: Perspiration. **—sweat of the brow:** Hard physical labor.

swindle: To obtain, by fraudulent means, something which belongs to another.

syllabus: An outline or general plan for a course of study.

amil: தமிழ் The ancient Dravidian language of the Tamils, a Caucasoid people of South India and Northern Sri Lanka, now living throughout the world. The official language of the state of Tamil Nadu, India.

tangle: A disorderly mass, as of hair, from which it is difficult to create order.

tantrum: A fit of uncontrolled anger, temper or rage.

tapestry: Something felt to resemble a richly and complexly designed cloth.

taut: Pulled or drawn tight; not slack.

tawdry: Gaudy and cheap; in poor taste.

teeming: Abounding; swarming; existing in great numbers.

temple: An edifice in a consecrated place dedicated to the worship of God or Gods. Hindus revere their temples as sacred, magical places in which the three worlds most consciously commune—structures especially built and consecrated to channel the subtle spiritual energies of inner-world beings.

tenacity: Persistence, resoluteness.

tenet: A principle, doctrine, or belief held as a truth, as by a group.

terse: Brief, succinct, concise.

testimony: A statement or other evidence in support of certain facts.

tether: A rope or chain to keep an animal restrained within certain bounds.

theologian: A scholar of religious doctrine.

thicket: A dense growth of shrubs or underbrush.

three worlds: The three worlds of existence, *triloka*, are the primary hierarchical divisions of the cosmos. 1) *Bhuloka:* "Earth world," the physical plane. 2) *Antarloka:* "Inner or in-between world," the subtle or astral plane. 3) *Sivaloka:* "World of Siva," and of the Gods and highly evolved souls; the causal plane, also called Karanaloka. See: *Sivaloka.*

thuravi: துறவி Tamil name for sannyasin. See: *sannyasa.*

timeless: Outside the condition of time, or not measurable in terms of time.

Tirumantiram: திருமந்திரம் "Holy incantation." The Nandinatha Sampradaya's oldest Tamil scripture; written ca 200 BCE by Rishi Tirumular. It is the earliest of the *Tirumurai* texts, and a vast storehouse of esoteric yogic and tantric knowledge. It contains the mystical essence of *raja yoga* and *siddha yoga,* and the fundamental doctrines of the 28 *Saiva Siddhanta Agamas.*

Tirumular: திருமூலர் An illustrious *siddha yogi* and *rishi* of the Nandinatha Sampradaya's Kailasa Parampara who came from the Himalayas (ca 200 BCE) to Tamil Nadu to compose the *Tirumantiram.* Tirumular was a disciple of Maharishi Nandinatha. See: *Tirumantiram, Kailasa Parampara.*

touchstone: A criterion by which genuineness or worth in a particular matter can be ascertained. Originally a kind of black stone formerly used to determine the purity of gold and silver.

tramp: A vagabond. A prostitute. A person regarded as promiscuous..

transcendent: Surpassing the limits of experience or manifest form. In Saiva Siddhanta, a quality of God Siva as Absolute Reality, the Self. Distinguished from immanent.

transgress: To overstep or break a law or ethical principle.

transition: That which leads from one thing to another; a linking, as between topics of a book, stages of life, etc.

tread: To walk upon or along.

trepidation: Shaking with fear; alarm; agitation.

trifling: Frivolous, insignificant.

trigger: To activate.

triumphant: Exulting, celebrating, rejoicing over a success or victory.

trivial: Insignificant.

Trojan War: Legendary reminiscences of a war waged by the Greeks against the city of Troy, probably around 1200 BCE.

True Being: In Saivite Hinduism, the true being of man (indeed, of all of existence) is seen as none other than God.

Truth: When capitalized, ultimate knowing which is unchanging. Lower case (truth): honesty, integrity, virtue.

typical: Representative, characteristic.

Unbaked clay pot: A pot prior to firing in a kiln, which would dissolve if water were poured into it.

uncharitable: Harsh, severe, ungenerous.

unchaste: Indulging in sexual intercourse with other than one's spouse.

unequivocally: Plainly, clearly, with no ambiguity.

unextinguished: Not extinguished; allowed to remain burning.

unfold: To open gradually, especially in stages.

uninquisitive: Disinclined to seek knowledge; disinterested in learning.

universal: Having to do with the universe; also, pertaining to everything in the universe, or to everything or everyone within a specified sphere.

universe: The sum total of physical manifestation, comprising all the galaxies, space between the galaxies, living beings, and all the forces that affect matter.

unleash: To release or set free; to remove restraints from.

unmindful: Careless, inattentive, heedless.

unpretentiousness: Lack of pretension or affectation; modesty.

unprovoked: Without provocation; uncalled-for; preceded by no apparent incitement; usually referring to a hostile act.

unremitting: Not stopping or slackening; persistent.

unrivaled: Matchless, peerless, unequalled.

unsavory: Unpleasant, offensive, immoral.

unscrupulous: Unprincipled, dishonest; unrestrained by the concept of dharma.

unswerving: Holding a straight course; never deviating from dharma.

untutored: Untaught.

Upanishad: उपनिषद् "Sitting near devotedly." The fourth and final portion of the *Vedas,* expounding the secret, philosophical meaning of the Vedic hymns. The *Upanishads* are a collection of profound texts which are the source of Vedanta and have dominated Indian thought for thousands of years. They are philosophical chronicles of *rishis* expounding the nature of God, soul and cosmos, exquisite renderings of the deepest Hindu thought.

uplift: To elevate or raise the level of (often used in a spiritual sense).

upright: Honest, honorable, pure in thought and conduct.

Vacant: Without an incumbent or occupant; unfilled.

valiance: Bravery, courage, strength, heroism.

vast: Huge; immense; great in extent; boundless.

Veda: वेद Wisdom. Sagely revelations comprising Hinduism's most authoritative scripture. They, along with the *Agamas*, are *shruti*, that which is "heard." The *Vedas* are a body of dozens of holy texts known collectively as the *Veda*, or as the four *Vedas: Rig, Yajur, Sama* and *Atharva*. In all they include over 100,000 verses, as well as additional prose. The oldest portions of the *Vedas* are thought to date back as far as 6,000 BCE. Written down in Sanskrit in the last few millennia, they are the worlds most ancient scriptures.

vegetarian: *Shakahara.* Of a diet which excludes meat, fish, fowl and eggs. Vegetarianism is a principle of health and environmental ethics that has been a keystone of Indian life for thousands of years.

venerate: To love or consider with respect and admiration; to revere.

verbiage: An excess of words; wordiness.

verdant: Green with growing things.

vernacular: Common, everyday manner of speaking; local dialect.

version: A specific presentation, interpretation, or translation of a particular work.

vestige: Trace or evidence of a thing's ever existing.

vibrant: Energetic, vital; full of life force.

vigilance: Watchfulness; being alert for any danger.

vigor: Vibrant physical and/or mental energy, strength & health.

vile: Morally bad; wicked; offensive.

vitality: Energy and vigor.

Vivekananda, Swami: (1863-1902) Disciple of Sri Ramakrishna, known for his missionary zeal and brilliant lectures around the world.

vying: Competing.

anton: Undisciplined, reckless, immoral. Lascivious, lustful; having no regard for chastity.

warp: The threads that run lengthwise in a woven fabric, crossed at right angles to the weft. *Warp and weft.*

weft: The threads (also called the *woof*) that run crosswise in a woven fabric, crossed at right angles to the warp.

well-winnowed: Carefully sifted (as with grain, in the wind) so as to eliminate the unnecessary elements, leaving only that which is valuable.

whip: To punish or chastise by repeated striking with a strap or rod; flog.

wile: Strategems; sly, deceitful ways of accomplishing one's desires.

will-o'-the-wisp: Anything that deludes or misleads by luring on.

wither: To lose vigor; weaken, languish.

witness: One who can give a firsthand account of something seen, heard, or experienced.

womankind: Women, spoken of as an entire group.

womb: In general, the environment in which something begins its growth and development.

wonder: A marvelous thing; a feeling of amazement. Also, to marvel or wish to know.

wondrous: Wonderful, marvellous; Inspiring awe, extraordinary, mirific.

worldly: Of, relating to, or devoted to the temporal world.

worshipful: Worthy of worship.

wrath: Violent anger; fury. Or, an action carried out with great anger or rage.

wreak: To inflict.

wretched: Miserable, abject, dismal.

ak: A wild, shaggy-haired ox *(Bos grunniens)* of the mountains of central Asia. A domesticated yak is used as a work animal or raised for meat and milk.

Yoga Sutras: Patanjali's most famous work, comprising 200 aphorisms delineating *ashtanga* (eight-limbed), *raja* (kingly) or *siddha* (perfection) yoga. Still today it is the foremost text on meditative yoga. See: *Patanjali.*

yoga: योग "Union." From *yuj,* "to yoke, harness, unite." The philosophy, process, disciplines and practices whose purpose is the yoking of individual consciousness with transcendent or divine consciousness.

Yogaswami: யோகசுவாமி "Master of *yoga.*" Sri Lanka's most renowned contemporary spiritual master (1872–1964), a *siddhar* revered by both Hindus and Buddhists. He was trained in and practiced *kundalini* yoga under the guidance of Satguru Chellappaswami, from whom he received *guru diksha.* Sage Yogaswami was in turn the *satguru* of Sivaya Subramuniyaswami, current preceptor of the Natha Sampradaya's Kailasa Parampara. Yogaswami conveyed his teachings in hundreds of songs, called *Natchintanai,* "good thoughts," urging seekers to follow dharma and realize God within. Four great sayings capsulize his message: *Thanai ari,* "Know thy Self by thyself;" *Sarvam Sivam Ceyal,* "Siva is doing it all;" *Sarvam Sivamaya,* "All is Śiva;" and Summa Iru, "Be still."

yogi: योगी One who practices yoga, especially *kundalini* or *raja* yoga.

yogini: योगिनी Feminine counterpart of yogi.

yuga: युग "Period, age." One of four ages which chart the duration of the world according to Hindu thought. They are: Satya (or Krita), Treta, Dvapara and Kali. In the first period, dharma reigns supreme, but as the ages revolve, virtue diminishes and ignorance and injustice increases. At the end of the Kali Yuga, in which we are now, the cycle begins again with a new Satya Yuga.

ealously: With great zeal; ardently, eagerly, enthusiastically, fervently.

Index

Attavanai

அட்டவணை

I

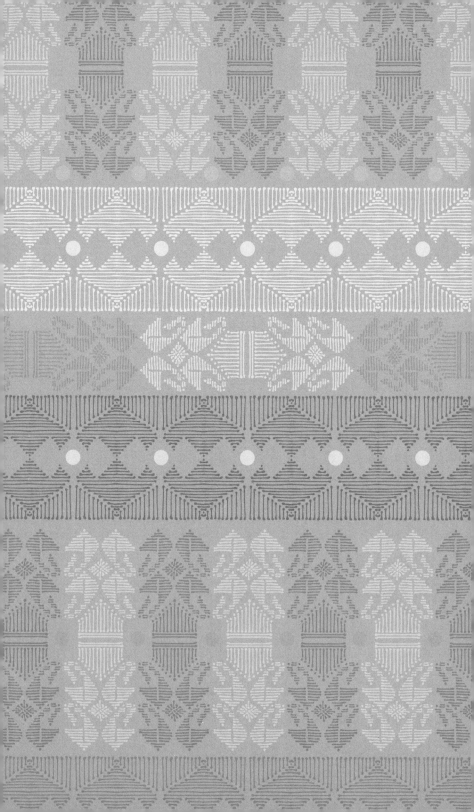

Resources

Thunai Noolkal

துணை நூல்கள்

Scripture and Sacred Literature

Rajagopalachari, C. (translator), *Kural, The Great Book of Thiruvalluvar.* Mumbai: Bharatiya Vidya Bhavan, 1965.

Natarajan, Dr. B. (translator), *Tirumantiram, A Tamil Scriptural Classic by Tirumular.* Mylapore, Madras: Sri Ramakrishna Math, 1991.

Panikkar, Raimond, *The Vedic Experience.* Delhi: Motilal Banarsidass, 1989.

Pope, G.U. and Drew, W.H., (translators) *Tirukkural.* Madras: The South India Saiva Siddhanta Works Publishing Society, 1981.

Sundaram, P.S., (translator) *Tiruvalluvar-The Kural.* New Delhi: Penguin Books (India) Limited, 1989.

Vanmikanathan, G. (translator), *The Thirukkural.* Thanjavoor, Thirupanandal: Sri Kasi Mutt, 1984.

Philosophy

Radhakrishnan, Dr. S., *Indian Philosophy* (two volumes). Oxford: Oxford University Press, 1923.

Subramuniyaswami, Sivaya, *Dancing with Siva: Hinduism's Contemporary Catechism.* Hawaii: Himalayan Academy, 1997.

Internet Resources

http://www.hindu.org/ha/ww/
Himalayan Academy Publications' online edition of *Weaver's Wisdom* in color; subscription to daily e-mail of verses from this translation.

http://www.hindu.org/books/
Himalayan Academy Publications, Modern Hindu texts by Satguru Sivaya Subramuniyaswami, as well as *Tirumantiram*, Siva Yogaswami's *Natchintanai* and *Words of our Master* and other Tamil resources.

http://www.hindu.org/today/
Today at Kauai Aadheenam, Satguru Sivaya Subramuniyaswami's daily inspirational voice message in English, Tamil, Malay and French.

http://members.xoom.com/thamhiz/
Thamhiz Thendril: Original Tamil verses of *Tirukural* and others.

http://magna.com.au/~prfbrown/
Mountain Man Graphics: This American English translation of *Tirukural* and other classic Tamil texts.

http://www.tamil.net/projectmadurai/
Thamizh Inaiyam's Project Madurai: Classic Tamil literature such as *Tirukural, Tirumantiram, Tiruvasagam,* and works by Auvaiyar.

http://www.tamilnation.org/literature.htm
Tamil National Foundation's Tamil Nation: Resources on Tamil language.

http://www.geocities.com/Athens/5180/index.html
Tamil Electronic Library: A vast collection of links to Tamil websites, electronic texts, language, literature and culture.

Colophon

Patippurai
பதிப்புரை

WEAVER'S WISDOM, ANCIENT PRECEPTS FOR A PERFECT LIFE, WAS RENDERED INTO AMERICAN ENGLISH OVER A PERIOD OF TWENTY-FOUR YEARS BY two of Gurudeva's designated successors. It was designed and produced by the *acharyas* and swamis of the Saiva Siddhanta Yoga Order at Kauai's Aadheenam on Hawaii's Garden Island, overlooking the Wailua River at the base of the extinct volcano Mount Waialeale. This second book in the Siddha Collection was edited and assembled using QuarkXPress on a network of PowerMac G3s. The text is set in Dominante 10 on 14. The Devanagari font is by Ecological Linguistics, and the Tamil font is by K. Srinivasan. Pages were output to film by BookCrafters in Chelsea, Michigan, and printed on 60# Enviro-text stock. Assistance with the glossary and proofreading was provided by R.V. Subramanian, Chamundi Sabanathan and Rajadeva Alahan, all three of California. The 108 pictures illustrating each chapter, along with the painting on page xx, are the work of Tiru A. Manivelu of Chennai. The cover art and the iamge of Lord Murugan opposite the title page are by Tiru S. Rajam of Chennai. The spiritual likeness of Saint Tiruvalluvar on the title page is the unique work of Tirumati Saroja Nagarathnam of Chennai, which she created by penning the weaver's 1,330 Tamil verses in microscopic size with colored inks. The oil portrait on the back cover was an inspired gift by India's renowned artist Sri Indra Sharma during his visit to Kauai in 1997. Indraji also did the portrait of Satguru Yogaswami on page iv. The cloth-like pattern graphics are the contribution of a gifted soul among our Saiva *sannyasin* order.

About Gurudeva

ONCE IN A WHILE ON THIS EARTH THERE ARISES A SOUL WHO, BY LIVING HIS TRADITION RIGHTLY AND WHOLLY, PERFECTS HIS PATH AND BECOMES A light to the world. Satguru Sivaya Subramuniyaswami is such a being, a living example of awakening and wisdom, a leader recognized worldwide as one of Hinduism's foremost ministers. In 1947, as a young man of 20, he journeyed to India and Sri Lanka and two years later was initiated into *sannyasa* by the renowned siddha yogi and worshiper of Siva, Jnanaguru Yogaswami of Sri Lanka, regarded as one of the 20th century's most remarkable mystics. For over five decades Subramuniyaswami, affectionately known as Gurudeva, has taught Hinduism to Hindus and seekers from all faiths. He is the 162nd successor of the Nandinatha Kailasa lineage and *satguru* of Kauai Aadheenam, a 51-acre temple-monastery complex on Hawaii's Garden Island. On this verdant Polynesian ashram on a river bank near the foot of an extinct volcano, he and his monastics live their cherished vision, following a contemplative and joyous existence, building a jewel-like white granite Siva temple, meditating together in the hours before dawn, then working, while rainbows fill the sky, to promote the Sanatana Dharma together through four areas of service: Saiva Siddhanta Church, Himalayan Academy, Hindu Heritage Endowment and HINDUISM TODAY international monthly magazine. Gurudeva is lauded as one of the strictest and most traditional gurus in the world. His Church nurtures its membership and local missions on five continents. The Academy serves, personally and through its magazine, books, courses and travel/study program, serious seekers and Hindus of all denominations. Gurudeva's mission, received from his *satguru*, is to protect, preserve and promote the Saivite Hindu religion as expressed through its three pillars: temples, *satgurus* and scripture. The congregation of Saiva Siddhanta Church is a disciplined, global fellowship of family initiates, monastics and students who follow the *sadhana marga,* the path of inner effort, yogic striving and personal transformation. Gurudeva is the hereditary guru of 2.5 million Sri Lankan Hindus. His is a Jaffna-Tamil-based organization which has branched out from his Sri Subramuniya Ashram in Alaveddy to meet the needs of the growing Hindu diaspora of this century. He has established a seven-acre monastery in Mauritius, which includes a public Spiritual Park. Gurudeva gently oversees more than 50 temples worldwide. Missionaries and teachers within the family membership provide counseling and classes in Saivism for children, youth and adults. HINDUISM TODAY is the influential, award-winning, international monthly magazine founded by Gurudeva in 1979. It is a public service of his monastic order, created to strengthen all Hindu traditions by uplifting and informing followers of the Sanatana Dharma everywhere. Gurudeva is author of more than 30 books unfolding unique and practical insights on Hindu metaphysics, mysticism and yoga. His Master Course lessons on Saivism, taught in many schools, are preserving the teachings among thousands of youths. Hindu Heritage Endowment is a public service trust founded by Gurudeva in 1995. It seeks to establish and maintain permanent sources of income for Hindu institutions worldwide. In 1986, New Delhi's World Religious Parliament named Gurudeva one of five modern-day Jagadacharyas, world teachers, for his international efforts in promoting and chronicling a Hindu renaissance. Then in 1995 it bestowed on him the title of Dharmachakra for his remarkable publications. The Global Forum of Spiritual and Parliamentary Leaders for Human Survival chose Subramuniya-swami as a Hindu representative at its unique conferences. Thus, at Oxford, England, in 1988, Moscow in 1990 and Rio de Janiero in 1992, he joined hundreds of religious, political and scientific leaders from all countries to discuss privately, for the first time, the future of human life on this planet. At Chicago's historic centenary Parliament of the World's Religions in September, 1993, Gurudeva was elected one of three presidents, along with Swami Chidananda Saraswati of the Rishikesh-based Divine Life Society and Kerala's Ammachi, Mata Amritanandamayi Ma, to represent Hinduism at the prestigious Presidents' Assembly, a core group of 25 men and women voicing the needs of world faiths. In 1996 Gurudeva upgraded the newspaper HINDUISM TODAY to a magazine, a quantum leap that placed it on newsstands everywhere, alongside *Newsweek, Time* and *India Today*. In 1997 he responded to the US President's call for religious opinions on the ethics of cloning from the Hindu point of view. Later that year, he spearheaded the 125th anniversary of Satguru Yogaswami and his golden icon's diaspora pilgrimage through many of the over 75 Sri Lanka temples and societies around the globe. In 1998, the Vishva Hindu Parishad of Kerala sent an envoy to Kauai to honor Gurudeva as the "Hindu Voice of the Century." Recently, Gurudeva has been a key member of Vision Kauai, a small group of community leaders that includes the Mayor, former Mayor, County Council members, and business and education leaders. They meet monthly to fashion the island's future for twenty years ahead, based on moral and spiritual values. If you ask people who know Gurudeva what is so special about him, they may point to his great peace, presence and centeredness, to his incredible power to inspire others toward their highest Self, to change their lives in ways that are otherwise impossible, to be an unfailing light on their path, to be a voice of Indian spiritual life, to bring the best of the East and the best of the West together for all seekers of Truth, to be a father and mother to all who draw near, a living example of the pure path taught by his guru and followed by his devoted *shishyas*.

You can visit Gurudeva's home page on the Web: www.hindu.org/gurudeva/ and hear his daily voice message at www.hindu.org/today/

There are a few unusual men who have had enough of the world and choose to dance, live and merge with Siva as Hindu monks.

These rare souls follow the path of the traditional Hindu monastic, vowed to poverty, humility, obedience, purity and confidence. They pursue the disciplines of *charya*, *kriya*, *yoga* and *jnana* that lead to Self Realization. Knowing God is their only goal in life. They live with others like themselves in monasteries apart from the world to worship, meditate, serve and realize the truth of the *Vedas* and *Agamas*. Guided by Satguru Sivaya Subramuniyaswami and headquartered at Kauai Aadheenam in Hawaii, USA, the Saiva Siddhanta Yoga Order is among the world's foremost traditional Hindu monastic orders, accepting candidates from every nation on Earth. Young men considering life's renunciate path who strongly believe they have found their spiritual master in Gurudeva are encouraged to write to him, sharing their personal history, spiritual aspirations, thoughts and experiences. Holy orders of *sannyasa* may be conferred in Gurudeva's order after ten to twelve years of training.

Satguru Sivaya Subramuniyaswami
Guru Mahasannidhānam, Kauai Aadheenam
107 Kaholalele Road, Kapaa, Hawaii 96746-9304 USA

*Hail, O sannyasin, love's embodiment! Does any power
exist apart from love? Diffuse thyself throughout the
happy world. Let painful māyā cease and never return.
Day and night give praise unto the Lord. Pour forth a
stream of songs to melt the very stones. Attain the sight
where night is not, nor day. See Śiva everywhere and rest
in bliss. Live without interest in worldly gain.
Here, as thou hast ever been, remain.*

YOGASWAMI'S NATCHINTANAI 228

The Mini-Mela Giftshop

For all our books, visit www.hindu.org/books/

Dancing with Śiva

Hinduism's Contemporary Catechism

This remarkable 1,008-page sourcebook covers every subject, answers every question and quenches the thirst of the soul for knowledge of God and the Self. Clearly written and lavishly illustrated, expertly woven with 600 verses from the *Vedas*, *Agamas* and other holy texts, 165 South Indian paintings, 40 original graphics, a 40-page timeline of India's history and a 190-page lexicon of English, Sanskrit and Tamil. A spiritual gem and great value at twice the price. *"The most comprehensive and sensitive introduction to the living spiritual tradition of Hinduism ...a feast for the heart and the mind (Georg Feuerstein)."* Fifth edition, 1997, 8.5" x 5.5", softcover (ISBN 0-945497-97-0), $29.85.

Living with Śiva

Hinduism's Contemporary Culture

Hindu culture is nowhere illumined better than in this collection of Satguru Sivaya Subramuniyaswami's honest, unflinching thoughts on every aspect of human life. These are given in the form of 365 sutras—spiritual rules for the lion-hearted, verses on how Hindus approach God, family life, sex, relationships, money, food, health, social protocol, worship and more. This book proclaims and clearly explains the ancient wisdom of how followers of Sanatana Dharma lived and interrelated with one another in the days when love and peace, respect and wisdom prevailed, and it shows how that spiritual life can and should be lived today. First edition, 1991, 8.5" x 5.5", 228 pages, illustrated, softcover (ISBN 0-945497-44-x), $8.95.

Merging with Śiva

Hinduism's Contemporary Metaphysics

Here is the ultimate text for the really serious seeker. It may well go down in history as the richest and most inspired statement of meditation and God Realization ever, in any language. Yet, it's user-friendly, easy to follow, sensible and nonacademic! *Merging with Śiva* is 365 daily lessons, one for each day of the year, about the core of your own being. It's about God, about the mystical realm of the fourteen chakras, the human aura, karma, force fields, thought and the states of mind, the two paths, *samadhi* and so much more. For the first time we include in this book the cream of Gurudeva's mystical inspired talk booklets, such as "The Self God," "The Clear White Light," "The River of Life" and many surprises for old-timers. Illustrated with fifty original South Indian paintings. First edition, 1999, 8.5" x 5.5," 1,408 pages, softcover (ISBN 0-945497-74-1), $39.75.

Loving Gaṇeśa

Hinduism's Endearing Elephant-Faced God

It began September 21, 1995, when an image of Ganesha in a New Delhi temple began sipping milk, a modern miracle soon witnessed by millions, in temples, shrines and homes worldwide. How timely that, just days before, Satguru Sivaya Subramuniyaswami had finished the 800-page sourcebook *Loving Gaṇeśa*. The book is simple, deep and practical, teaching how Ganesha's grace can be attained by devotion, song, prayer and meditation. "Lord Ganesha comes to life through the pages of this inspired masterpiece. *Loving Gaṇeśa* makes approaching Ganesha easy and inspiring (The Mystic Trader)." First Edition, 1996, 8.5" x 5.5", 794 pages, beautifully illustrated with classical Rajput paintings, softcover (ISBN 0-945497-64-4), $24.85.

The Master Course

Śaivite Hindu Religion

What every Hindu parent needs: intelligent, nonviolent, traditional texts for their kids—an illustrated, seven-book series called *The Master Course*, teaching philosophy, culture and family life. Based on the holy *Vedas*, this course is the loving work of Sivaya Subramuniyaswami, based on the *Saiva Neri* course from the Sri Lankan school system. An excellent resource for educators and parents, it explains the "why" of each belief and practice in simple terms in three languages. "A commendable, systematically conceived course useful to one and all with special significance to fortunate children who shall be led on the right path (Sri Sri Sri Tiruchi Mahaswamigal, Bangalore, India)." Book One (5- to 7-year-old level) is available in a Hindi-Tamil-English edition. Softcover, 8.5" x 5.5", 170 pages, $12.95. Book Two (6- to 8-year-old level), English-Tamil-Malay, 196 pages, $12.95.

The Vedic Experience

Back when we were gathering Vedic verses for *Dancing with Śiva*, we could hardly believe our eyes when we came upon this brilliant anthology from the Vedic *Samhitas, Brahmanas, Aranyakas* and *Upanishads* and other scriptures. This Vedic epiphany tells the story of the universal rhythms of nature, history and humanity. The translation and abundant commentary are the work of renaissance thinker Raimon Panikkar—the fruit of twelve years of daily *sadhana* in Varanasi between 1964 and 1976 while he lived above a Siva temple on the Holy Ganga. He considers it perhaps his most significant literary contribution. This classic makes the *Vedas* available to all. Motilal Banarsidass, Delhi, 1977, smythe-sewn and case bound, cloth cover, 8.5" x 5.5", 1,000 pages, $41.

Hinduism Today

The International Monthly Magazine

Since 1979 Hinduism Today has been the fore-most news magazine on Sanatana Dharma worldwide. For Hindus and non-Hindus alike, it covers the life, experience and ways of a faith in renaissance in communities from New Delhi to New York, from Moscow to Durban. Coverage includes religion, contro-versy, *yoga*, vegetarianism, meditation, non-violence, environmental ethics, pilgrimage, interfaith harmony, family life, and more. Re-porting from the spectrum of Hindu lineages, leaders and personalities, it is clear, articulate and stunning in full-color photos and art. Bring classical culture and contemporary wisdom to your fingertips each month. US$3.95; CAN$4.95 • ISSN 0896-0801; UPC: 0-74470-12134-3. See order form for subscription rates.

Lemurian Scrolls

Angelic Prophecies Revealing Human Origins

Enliven your spiritual quest with this clairvoyant rev-elation of mankind's journey to Earth millions of years ago from the Pleiades and other planets to fur-ther the soul's unfoldment. Learn about the ensuing challenges and experiences faced in evolving from spiritual bodies of light into human form and the profound practices followed in ancient Lemuria. These angelic prophecies, read by Sivaya Subramu-niyaswami from *akashic* records written two million years ago, will over-whelm you with a sense of your divine origin, purpose and destiny and mo-tivate a profound rededication to your spiritual quest. An extraordinary metaphysical book which answers the great questions: Who am I? Where did I come from? Where am I going? First Edition, 1998, 7" x 10", 400 pages, beautifully illustrated with original drawings, smythe-sewn and case bound with printed color cover (ISBN 0-945497-70-9), $29.85.

Monks' Cookbook—*Vegetarian Recipes from Kauai's Hindu Monastery*

South Indian ashrams serve the finest cruelty-free meals enjoyed anywhere, and Kauai's Hindu Monastery carries on the 6,000-year-old tradition. Now the monks have shared their secret collection of recipes, gathered over the years and perfected in the Islands made famous by, wouldn't you know, Captain Cook! Enhance all your meals with this cornucopia of Jaffna-style and Indian dishes from around the world for daily meals and elaborate festivals. Also included is a 30-page ready reference on the unique *ayurvedic* qualities of a vast variety of spices, grains, fruits and vegetables. First Edition, 1997, 8.5" x 11", 104 pages, lightly illustrated, durable paper, maroon spiral binding, softcover (ISBN 0-945497-71-7), $16.95.

Hawaiian-Grown Rudraksha Beads

Here is a 36-bead strand, packed with Hawaii's sublime life-energy. The beads, gathered fresh each year from the Rudraksha forest floor at Kauai's Hindu Monastery, lovingly cleaned an strung, are five-faced and roughly 3/4-inch in diameter, with small gold beads in between. $54.

"Aum Namasivaya" Bracelet

With this handsome piece of Indian jewelry for men or women, you can wear the most sacred Saiva mantra, "Aum Namasivaya," all day as a reminder of God's grace at work in your life. Best quality, made in India from silver, copper and brass, with the mantra in Sanskrit. Band is five-eighths inches wide. Excellent for gifts. $30. Gold plated: $59.85.

Mini-Mela Giftshop Order Form

☐ Please send me a free literature packet.

☐ I consider myself a devotee of Satguru Sivaya Subramuniyaswami.

☐ I wish to subscribe to HINDUISM TODAY.

   ☐ 1 year, $39   ☐ 2 years, $74   ☐ Lifetime, $800

I would like to order: ☐ *Dancing with Śiva*, $29.85   ☐ *Living with Śiva*, $8.95
☐ *Merging with Śiva*, $39.75   ☐ *Loving Gaṇeśa*, $24.95   ☐ *Vedic Experience*, $41
☐ *Lemurian Scrolls*, $29.85   ☐ *Monks' Cookbook*, $16.95
☐ *Śaivite Hindu Religion*, $12.95 ea: ☐ Book 1; ☐ Book 2   ☐ Rudraksha mala, $39
☐ "Aum Namasivaya" Bracelet, $30; ☐ Gold plated, $59.85

   Prices are in U.S. currency. Add 20% for postage and handling in USA and
   foreign, $1.50 minimum. Foreign orders are shipped sea mail unless oth-
   erwise specified and postage is paid. For foreign airmail, add 50% of the
   merchandise total for postage.

☐ My payment is enclosed.   Charge to: ☐ MasterCard   ☐ Visa   ☐ Amex

Card number: _____

Expiration, month: _____ year: _____ Total of purchase: $ _____

Name on card: [PLEASE PRINT] _____

Signature: _____

Address: [PLEASE PRINT] _____

_____

Phone: _____ Fax: _____

E-mail: _____

Mail, phone, fax or e-mail orders to:

Himalayan Academy Publications, Kauai's Hindu Monastery, 107 Kaholalele
Road, Kapaa, Hawaii 96746-9304 USA. Phone (US only): 1-800-890-1008; outside US:
1-808-822-7032 ext. 238; Fax: 1-808-822-3152; E-mail: books@hindu.org;
World Wide Web: www.hindu.org/books/

Also available through the following. (Write or call for prices.)

Sanathana Dharma Publications, Bukit Panjang Post Office, P. O. Box 246,
   Singapore 916809. Phone: 65-362-0010; Fax: 65-442-3452;
   E-mail: sanatana@mbox4singnet.com.sg

Saiva Siddhanta Church of Mauritius, La Pointe, Rivière du Rempart,
   Mauritius, Indian Ocean. Phone: 230-412-7682; Fax: 230-412-7177.

Iraivan Temple Carving Site, P.O. Box No. 4083, Vijayanagar Main,
   Bangalore, 560 040. Phone: 91-80-839-7118; Fax: 91-80-839-7119;
   E-mail: jiva@giasbg01.vsnl.net.in

Om Vishwa Guru Deep Hindu Mandir, Europe: Phone/Fax: 361-3143504;
   E-mail: ervin@mail.matav.hu

Weaver's Wisdom, the latest American English translation of *Tirukural*, is by far one of the best, if not the best, that has appeared in this century. Satguru Sivaya Subramuniyaswami has introduced each of the sections. He has also provided guidance on how to benefit from a study of the volume. He recommends daily chanting of the Pranava Mantra Aum thrice, then opening the book at random and focusing on the verses that appear. ¶The authors have succeeded in providing the additional dimension of an excellent portrayal of Tiruvalluvar, his ideal relationship with his wife Vasuki, worthy of emulation, and the functioning of various classes of society 2,200 years ago. What was written about the guidelines for organizing the various facets of life in an ethical framework then are valid and relevant today. This will certainly continue to be so in the next millennium, which is about to dawn. ¶The text is composed in utmost simplicity, direct, easily understandable and yet profound. The illustrations are numerous and help to faithfully present an understanding of the society during Tiruvalluvar's period. The present efforts in Tamil Nadu to honor Tiruvalluvar are presented in photographs with picturesque and graphic detail. The monuments that have been erected provide testimony to the devotion of Tamils to Tiruvalluvar. ¶This book will be of value to Tamils, wherever they may be, to develop deep and abiding ties with their parent heritage. This book should ideally, indeed, become part of compulsory reading and be a daily companion to householders, high school children, college students, adults engaged in various walks of life and elders. Readers of this book, whichever culture, country or continent they come from, will gain a great friend, philosopher and guide in Tiruvalluvar.

Tiru A. Alagappan, Founding Member, New York Ganesha Temple; Former Director of the Natural Resources Division, Department of Economic and Social Affairs, United Nations Headquarters; New York, USA

Weaver's Wisdom, more popularly known as *Tirukural*, a 2,200-year-old Dravidian classic on the art and science of living, though written by Saint Tiruvalluvar, does not belong to India or the Tamil-speaking people in particular. It is the permanent possession of the human race. The saint's message is not meant for one age or for one country, but for all time and for all mankind. His catholic spirit rose above all religious denominations and sects. His vision was not clouded by dogmas or prejudices of any kind. His great work is perfect in form, profound in thought and full of nobleness of sentiment and earnestness of moral purpose. It is a practical guide that applies to everyday matters and common concerns. This work is praised by the Tamil people as the Tamil Veda. ¶The several translations of the Kural in many Indian languages and in almost all the important languages of the world, like English, French and Latin, bear testimony to its universal appeal to all nations. Recently I was pleasantly surprised to come across a translation of this great treatise in the

Fijian language, which is a laudable venture. However, it is a great pity that such an immortal classic has never been known in the Western world. ¶Translating an original masterpiece in any language is a task beset with many difficulties and problems, notwithstanding the translator's linguistic capacities and excellent scholarship. Very often, the translations are feeble and do not at all do justice to the merits of the original. On the contrary, the translators deform its grand thoughts by giving them a stilted and unnatural expression. Again, several obscure points in the original are not made clear in translation, and the imaginative translator bypasses this difficulty by taking shelter in pompous and meaningless words. ¶Above all, each *kural* is a couplet of the intricate *venpa* meter in Tamil. Each verse is extremely short and packed with lofty thoughts. Saint Tiruvalluvar has never used an irrelevant or unnecessary word. Its brevity is its strength. This adds to the difficulty for the translator. ¶This American English translation by Satguru Sivaya Subramuniyaswami of Hawaii is a masterpiece. This difficult task was successfully completed by the revered Swamiji and his devoted disciples after two decades of thorough preparation. This monumental work had taken many years for refining, polishing and perfecting. Many things have been achieved in this world by great people making hard efforts coupled with the labor of genius. But the Swamiji's achievement is the result of intense *tapasya* and total surrender to the Divine. He has not only understood the meaning of the *Kural* in its entirety but has lived it all through his life. The striking feature of the translation is that it is perfectly accurate and brings out the true spirit of the original composition. The subtle and essential meanings are clearly explained in modern American English. ¶To bring out an excellent, accurate, clear translation of the *Kural,* written twenty-two centuries ago in classical Tamil, is a superhuman *sadhana.* The translators have done their work after long hours of meditation on Saint Tiruvalluvar. Unless one goes to higher levels of consciousness, Tiruvalluvar's subtle meanings and insight cannot be caught. Such a work as this could not have been written without pure intuition, a psychic awakening and the saint's blessings. This work has the sanction and seal of a divine power, which guides the steps of sincere seekers of Truth. Another redeeming feature of the translation is that it is couched in the language of the present day, the idiom of the age. Archaic forms of expression have been carefully avoided, and it will now reach an even wider audience. Anything that would be cumbersome for the average reader is not used in the translation. The language is easy-flowing, lucid and inspiring. ¶*Weaver's Wisdom* is divided in eight sections. Every section begins with a beautiful introduction by Gurudeva, Subramuniyaswami, in which he gives the reader briefly and clearly a succinct summary of the themes dealt with. This is of inestimable value and help to the student. It is very interesting to note that in Section III (The Way of the Renunciate) Gurudeva has most appropriately included the-never-to-be-forgotten "Song of the Sannyasin," composed by the illustrious Hindu monk, Swami Vivekananda, a true *sannyasin* who not only preached Vedanta but lived Vedanta. Gurudeva was deeply moved by Vivekananda's shining example of service and renunciation. ¶Gurudeva has explained the meaning of the much misunderstood concepts of karma and destiny with remarkable terseness and lucidity. He says clearly that it is wrong to think of karma in terms of what is understood by the words *fatalism* or *destiny*. Karma is the unalterable law of effect following previous causes. The word a Hindu uses for fate or destiny is *vidhi*. In the words of Gurudeva, "Karma is not fate, for man acts with free will, creating his own destiny." ¶The choice of the title of this work, *Weaver's Wisdom*, is also very significant. It sheds an interesting light on the saint's earthly and spiritual life. Tiruvalluvar was a humble weaver by birth and profession. At the same time he was a wonderful weaver of lofty thoughts in bewitching language, and he helped millions of people to solve their problems and sorrows of life. As Gurudeva says, "Many times the subject of one chapter's last verse will become the transition to the next chapter's first, like one thread tied to another to continue the weaving." The weaver has created the tapestry of life with the rich-colored threads of Virtue and Wealth.

Sri S. Harihara Sharma, B.A., Chief Priest, Sri Murugan Temple, Vancouver, Canada; Former Religious Programme Producer, Sri Lanka Broadcasting Corporation

I frequently quote from the *Tirukural* in my talks. This is because I regard this work by Tiruvalluvar as one of the most masterful compilations of proverbs that exists today. Though it may be an ancient text, it has never been more relevant to modern life. It contains all the wisdom necessary to guide every step of one's life. To those who apply these proverbs consistently, sure success in every aspect of life is guaranteed. I myself have long wanted to translate the text from Tamil in such a way that it will be more easily accessible and comprehensible to Westerners. Thankfully, Sri Sivaya Subramuniya Swamigal has completed this mammoth task and in doing so rendered an incomparable service to humanity. I congratulate him and send my prayers and blessings to all the sincere seekers who allow the *Weaver's Wisdom* to guide their lives. Om shanti.

His Holiness Sri Sri Swami Satchidananda, Founder and Spiritual Head of Satchidananda Ashram; Founder of the Light of Truth Universal Shrine (LOTUS); Yogaville, Virginia

Weaver's Wisdom, already translated into fourteen different languages, conveys the message in current, simple, elegant, effective style to the English-speaking world for probably another 2,000 years.

Tiru S. Kumarakulasingam, Former Assistant Commissioner of Education of Jaffna, Sri Lanka; Surrey, England

This book is like a key to the Kingdom of God. Whoever reads and follows its teachings should reach the lotus feet of the Almighty without doubt. All those living in this world, which is immersed in the sea of sadness, will reach permanent eternal bliss in this birth itself by using this book as a boat. I consider Satguru Sivaya Subramuniyaswami, as an *avatara* for having undertaken this great task. There is no doubt that it is the saint himself who is working through Gurudeva to perform this great task. May Saint Tiruvalluvar shower his grace on this entire universe to bestow permanent peace.

His Holiness Dr. Swami R.K. Murugesu, Founder, Sri Lankatheshwarar Deyana Mander, Nuwara Eliya, Sri Lanka

After Tamil Nadu and Sri Lanka, North America is reputed to have the largest Tamil population. Though efforts are taken, especially in Canada by the government, to teach Tamil language to the Tamil children, it is a very sad fact that the majority of them have no inclination at all to learn the language, let alone gain the proficiency to read and understand our glorious literary heritage. It is the sacred duty of every Tamil parent to instill certain ideals in the minds of our youngsters. Of these ideals the ones we consider supreme are to show respect for our culture, to cherish the traditions that we have inherited, to practice the values we consider sacred and to be aware of our roots. To achieve this our youth must have access to our proud literary possessions which are second to none in their resplendence and content. ¶How can they have access to our literary masterpieces if their Tamil language skills are totally inadequate to read and to understand them? So it can only be done through translations very loyal to the original. Satguru Sivaya Subramuniyaswami, Guru Mahasannidhanam of Kauai Aadheenam, has aptly endeared himself with the task of translating into American English one of the greatest if not the greatest poetic masterpieces, *Tirukural*, for which Tamils will remember him for many years to come. *Tirukural* is hailed a literary work of art by religious dignitaries of all faiths, as well as atheists, philosophers, politicians and social reformers as espousing their mandate and considered as sacred and enchanting as the *Holy Bible, Bhagavad Gita, Holy Koran* and *The Prophet*. The greatness of Tiruvalluvar's work is such that it will never be irrelevant or outmoded at any time, in any culture, faith or conviction. ¶The translation is specifically done to offer our youngsters in particular a glimpse of *Tirukural* in simple English, easy to understand. Though the primary target is the youth, since this translation adheres very much to the original, even the elders could understand better the intuited meaning if they read the translation, as the original may be sometimes confusing because of its brevity and the fact that in Tamil a word has several meanings, which vary very often with context. In its simplicity, there is no ambiguity at all in this translation! ¶I strongly suggest that every household should possess a copy of this gem and read it to and with the children every day after prayers and get them to memorize these axioms, at least one or two a day. This will later guide them at every phase of their life as this enchanting work dwells deep into the insights of life and will enable them to be good citizens. We, the Tamil parents living all over the world in general and North America in particular, owe a sense of deep gratitude to Satguru Sivaya Subramuniyaswami and his *sannyasins* for this magnificent production purported to help every child not only of Tamil descent, not only those of Asian origin, but existing all over the world to learn to know how best they could live as better humans and be good citizens of the world.

Ponniah Kanagasabapathy, Multicultural Consultant, Toronto District School Board; Former Principal, Mahajana College, Tellippallai, Sri Lanka; Former Inspector of Schools, Sokoto, Nigeria; North York, Ontario

The title of the book is both topical and relevant, not only for the devotees of Shiva but also for all mankind, as a significant section of youth is engulfed by a drug-taking culture; the home where peace and tranquility should prevail has now been destabilized; and mores and ethical values have flown through the window in man's relentless hunt for his material well-being. In such a scenario, the ancient wisdom of the Tamil Saivites as expounded by the moral philosopher and Saint Tiruvalluvar is now being offered to the English-speaking world under the title *Weaver's Wisdom, Ancient Precepts for a Perfect Life*. It is hoped that every reader of this book would be transported "back to basics." ¶That the teachings of moral and ethical values propagated more than two thousand years ago are still relevant today is a poor testimony of man's spiritual progress in the past two millennia during which he has made phenomenal progress in harnessing the coarse external forces of nature for the satisfaction of his physical needs, but at the same time has permitted stagnancy in the development of his inner, finer self both morally and spiritually. *Weaver's Wisdom*, written in American English, is poised to fill the void left empty until now by the lack of a proper rendering of the Tamil-language classic, *Tirukural*. It is my hope and prayer that the ever-hungry American people for new ideas that had made America the most advanced nation in the world in material wealth would mull over these *Tirukural* couplets and progress toward the most spiritually advanced nation. ¶In Malaysia today, prominence is being given to *Tirukural*. The Tamil News on channel two of the national television ends its news program with a recital of a couplet from the *Tirukural* with a brief exposition of the meaning of the couplet. In addition, the Indian Studies Department of University Malaya had in 1967 published the *Tirukural* in the Malay language, entitled *Tirukural–Sastera Kelasik Tamil Yang Agong (Tirukural–A Revered Tamil Classic Literature)*, translated by Ismail Hussein. ¶It gives me great pleasure to congratulate His Holiness Satguru Sivaya Subramuniyaswami for having published *Weaver's Wisdom*. Much effort has been expended spanning a period of two decades to translate and publish this highly venerated book of the Tamils. The moral teachings of the *Tirukural* are even today the guiding light for the Saivite Tamil. *Weaver's Wisdom* is only one of many gems that His Holiness has extracted from the depths of ancient writings. His Holiness has not only excavated them but also polished them to be acceptable to a modern world in a language suited for a vastly enlarged readership.

Tiru Perampalam Saravanamuthu of Kuala Lumpur, Malaysia; President, Selangor Wilayah Persekutuan Ceylon Saivites Association; Chairman, First National Malaysian Saiva Siddhanta Seminar, 1983

To comment on this holy book *Tirukural,* translated into modern American English from the holy devotional Tamil language, at the instance of the great Satguru Sivaya Subramuniyaswamigal, the 162nd Jagadacharya of the Nandinatha Sampradaya's Kailasa Parampara, my spiritual master, Mahasannidhanam of Kauai Aadheenam of Hawaii, "is like carrying coal to Newcastle." It is an accepted fact that the Tamil language is the Gods' language given to the Tamils by Lord Ganesha. The richness, devotion, knowledge, art, music, yoga, literature, etc., can only be enjoyed by those who have studied the very most ancient Tamil language. It is as old as Saivism. It has stood the test of times, such as wars, earthquakes and foreign invasion. Surely and certainly *Weaver's Wisdom* will become a handbook to those interested in a humble and modest life.

Dr. Pundit K.N. Navaratnam, M.A.F.A., F.A.A.; Jyotisha Marthand and National Astrologer of Australia; devotee of Satguru Siva Yogaswami; Sivathondan Center; Hallam, Australia

I thought about the question, "Which is superior, Sanskrit or Tamil?" Sanskrit and Tamil are equal in their greatness. We cannot say that the one is superior to the other. The reason is that the *Vedas* are in Sanskrit, and now in Tamil we have the *Kural.* If there were nothing equal to the *Vedas* in Tamil, Sanskrit should have been said to be superior. Now the *Kural* is present in Tamil as the equal of the *Vedas.* Both languages, Sanskrit and Tamil, are now seen to be equally great.

His Holiness Jagadguru Sri Sankaracharya Swami Chandrashekharendra Saraswathi, Sri Kanchi Kamakoti Peetam; Kanchipuram, Tamil Nadu, India, from his book, *The Vedas.*

Greater than the "maker" of the light may be the one who recognises the value of the light and holds it for all to see! In this context, Satguru Sivaya Subramuniyaswami is playing an invaluable role in spreading further the knowledge of the ages! I was amazed that there are already five translations into English of the *Tirukural* and this is the sixth. (Perhaps there may be more!) But what is significant is again the holder of the light! There can be little doubt that when a being of Satguru's stature translates and releases this book on the "Weavers Wisdom," it will witness a surge of interest as never before, on the greatness of *Tirukural*. ¶With hands raised in prayer I would like to urge Satguru to persuade all Indian families whose mother tongue is Tamil, especially those living outside India and Sri Lanka to go back to their Noble Traditions, Religion, Aspiration and Culture (TRAC), for it is within this TRAC that all the values of life are enshrined. ¶The sayings of Tiruvalluvar and Mother Auvaiyar have all the values that mankind needs to live noble lives. Can children be taught to memorise some of these sayings in original Tamil, and with full understanding of their meaning in English; these will be like giving the future generations golden torches, or compasses to guide them through the path of life! ¶When a giant moves, all take notice, if a spiritual giant like Satguru moves, people will take notice, only there must be others who are prepared to take up smaller torches to hold the light for the children and youth of today. Only if other readers of the works of Satguru are motivated to take pro-active action to uphold and spread Hindu TRAC, can the Hindu and Tamil TRAC withstand the negative impact of the forces of so called modernisation and globalisation! ¶I pray that those who read the Weaver's Wisdom and other works done by Satguru Sivaya Subramuniyaswami are inspired to take the torch to spread the light. If those who read these, and possibly ninety percent will be adults, merely read and put these books back on the shelf, then the noble efforts of this great soul will not find its full flower. The most noble thing that those who wish to honour Satguru for his contribution can do, is to take this light he is offering (and others he has offered) and spread this among the Tamil and Hindu children and youth of the world. A noble soul like Satguru will not want our praise, he is beyond these petty things humans crave for; what he would want is for the light that he has lit to be ignited in thousands, nay millions of other hearts. This is how devotees of great souls can honour their Guru! I thank Satguru most humbly for having given me the honour and grace to have contributed these words to this magnificent effort.

Dato J. Jagadeesan, Advisor to the Sathya Sai Central Council of Malaysia; Co-founder and Co-chairman of the Hindu TRAC Programme; Former Deputy Director General, Malaysian Industrial Development Authority; Kuala Lumpur, Malaysia

Apart from the privilege and honor of this opportunity in help-ing with the dissemination of the masterpiece of Tamil litera-ture, which is a gift to humanity from my native culture, I feel drawn to this task by my long conviction that the *Kural's* wis-dom, which transcends time and place, is particularly needed to guide young and old alike who are growing up in alien countries and in India, itself without direction from our an-cient culture. For more than two decades now I have been presenting English translations of *Kural* to graduating students in the US, with added comments on *Kural's* relevance in shaping one's conduct. The book I have used most often is the selection and translation by C. Rajagopalachari, *Kural*, pub-lished by Bhavan's Books, crisp, clear, concise. Now I will have one more gem to share with young students. ¶It is a matter of great satisfaction that Weaver's Wisdom suc-ceeds so well in presenting the essence of the *Kural* in simple understandable English of current usage. That the true spirit, import and content of the original are faithful-ly preserved in this effort without aberrations, alterations or intrusions is particular-ly welcome and praiseworthy. ¶As much as for the translation, if not more, readers will forever be grateful to the author for the detailed introductions he has crafted for the various sections of the book. ¶It is also noteworthy and very pleasing that the history and culture of Tamil Nadu, the Tamil people and the Tamil language of India are introduced in all their relevant aspects throughout the book. With the author's ardent admiration fully evident, these discussions serve to place *Weaver's Wisdom* in proper perspective against the background of its origin in the ancient Tamil culture. ¶The book should very well be an inspiration, not just to the Tamilian diaspora, but to all people, to live up to the high ideals and potential of human nature and progress. That indeed is the mission of the Satguru.

Dr. R.V. Subramanian, Ph.D., Greenbelt, Maryland, USA; Retired Professor, Washington State University, Pullman

I bestow all my blessings to you for your effort in bringing out the publication of the sacred *Kural*—the first 108 chapters—into American English. *Weaver's Wisdom*, your twenty years ef-fort, will really get a prominent place as the gem in the West-ern world and among the Tamils, irrespective of religion, all over the world. We, the Nallai Thirugnanasambanthar Ad-heenam of Jaffna, Sri Lanka, wish you all the best of health and all God's power to continue a life of spiritual service throughout the world.

His Holiness Srilasri Somasundara Gnanasambhantha Paramacharya Swamigal, Guru Mahasannidhanam, Nallai Thirugnanasambanthar Adheenam; Nallur, Jaffna, Sri Lanka

We deeply appreciate the earnest effort of Satguru Sivaya Sub-ramuniyaswami in the propagation of Saiva Siddhanta princi-ples and are very happy about his interest in translating se-lected valuable Tamil scriptures into American English. Swami-gal's recognition of the immense value of the 2,200-year-old masterpiece has resulted in the translation of the eternal Tamil classic, *Tirukural*. The book deals with all the principles that en-compass human life. Not only is it applicable to people who speak Tamil, but also it belongs to the whole world. We hope the book will be wide-ly popular, enabling all the globe to read it with interest and adopt the eternal prin-ciples in their lives. We congratulate the two monastics who have translated it from Tamil, and the Tamil Indian artist who has illustrated the chapters. We pray to Gnanama Nataraja Peruman for the book's successful distribution.

His Holiness Sri Sri Sri Sivaprakasa Pandarasannadhi Adheenakarthar Avargal, Tiruvavaduthurai Adheenam; Tiruvavaduthurai, South India

Sri Satguru Sivaya Subramuniyaswami had been chosen by his guru, the Sage of Jaffna, to enlighten with sublime thoughts the West in particular and all others living in this universe. In the coming years, what is righteousness will be questioned by many. This book will be a guiding lamp to all those who have such doubts. May Lord Shiva bless us all to lead a perfect, har-monious life is our humble prayer to Him.

Swami Chidrupananda, Spiritual Head of Ramakrishna Sri Sarada Sevashrama; Point Pedro, Jaffna, Sri Lanka

The fact that Gurudeva has identified *Tirumantiram* and *Tirukural* as twin texts par excellence for spiritual progress and mundane life speaks volumes on the uniqueness and univer-sality of these scriptures. Gurudeva has not only studied and translated *Tirumantiram* into English years back, but has ac-cepted the text as an authentic source for his spiritual experi-ences and pursuits. It is not exaggeration that Gurudeva has been spreading the message of *Tirumantiram* all over the globe over the years. Now Gurudeva has taken up the translation of *Tirukural*, popu-larly known as the Tamil Veda. Since it is rendered in English, the work will surely at-tract global attention. *Tirukural* is addressed not to a restricted race or region, but to the human race at large. The Tamils feel proud of Gurudeva's emphasis on universal brotherhood and human solidarity in addition to the ultimate goal of human life, the liberation from the bonds and merging with the Godhead.

Dr. V. Ganapati Sthapati, Traditional Architect, Builder and Sculptor; Chennai, Tamil Nadu, India; Founder & Researcher: Vastu Vedic Research Foundation; Chief Editor: *Vastu Purusha*

This English translation of the first two parts of *Tirukural* is a very good and valuable production by Satguru Sivaya Subramuniyaswamiji of Hawaii, with the assistance of a few disciples. It makes good and interesting reading, slightly on the explanatory side, in American English, to facilitate the average American to absorb and internalize the goodness projected systematically in these couplets by the great sage, Valluvar. The get up of the volume, too, is appropriate, with suitable introductory remarks by the Swamiji and effective illustrations, harking back to the images of the Tamil country of two millennia ago. I am sure this noble endeavor will achieve the purpose for which the Swamiji intends it. My respects to Satguru Sivaya Subramuniyaswamiji, who is doing great work for the people in propagating "Anbe Sivam," as well as the great Tamil works, such as *Tirukural*.

Dr. N. Mahalingam, B.Sc., F.I.E., Tamil Scholar; Chairman, Sakthi Group of Companies; Chennai, Tamil Nadu, India

His Grace, Jagadguru Subramuniyaswami of Kauai Aadheenam, Hawaii, has placed the Tamil-speaking world in his debt in presenting the timeless *Tirukural* anew, as an indispensable text, to enable men and women, governments and peoples to lead a perfect life. Human perfection is indeed the ultimate end and purpose of human life. Human perfection is the aim of education the world over. Whether mankind attains perfection or not, it should at least strive toward perfection. The Jagadguru's two American swamis have taken twenty years to fulfill the wishes of Gurudeva, to enrich the world with the time-tested truths of Tamil wisdom woven by a weaver named Tiruvalluvar. This is indeed a great accomplishment, a tremendous task undertaken with love and devotion. The classical scholar Juan Mascaro of Oxford took twenty-five years to translate the *Bhagavad Gita* into English so that no inner meaning of any Sanskrit term was lost in translation. The epigrammatic excellence of the couplets of the *Kural* is difficult to translate into any language, whether in prose or in poetry. It is often claimed by academics that a translation that is beautiful is often not faithful, and a translation that is faithful to the original is often not beautiful. This is an academic fallacy! Nevertheless, the two American translators of the *Kural* have succeeded in producing a very readable translation of the original text without loss of meaning. ¶The Jagadguru has in his introduction clearly stated the importance of the *Tirukural* and its reflection of Hindu religion, culture and civilization as it was some 2,000 years ago. In South India, Tamil and Saivism have been one and indivisible. It comes as no surprise, therefore, that Gurudeva has chosen to publish an English translation of the *Tirukural*, as it is the bedrock of Tamil religion, culture and civilization. Even the venerable Rishi Tirumular claimed that "God had created him in order that he compose Tamil." Both Tamil and Saivism find elaboration in both the texts, the *Tirukural* and the *Tirumantiram*. Today the *Tirukural* has attained a scriptural standing in South India as the Tamil *Veda*. This timeless Tamil classic will no doubt continue to excite and exercize the minds and enable the lives of men and women for generations to come. The letter and the spirit of the *Kural* must be illumined by the life an individual leads in this world. Those who preach it must endeavor to practice it. The Jagadguru, as a world teacher, has reintroduced the *Kural* as *Weaver's Wisdom* for all mankind, urging us to all learn and live by its truths and attain perfection.

> **Dr. S.M. Ponniah, Professor, INTI College; Member of the National Commission on Moral Education; Advisor to the Malaysian Hindu Sangam; Kuala Lumpur, Malaysia**

 Tens of thousands of years ago great Hindu sages unfolded the knowledge from within themselves to mankind. Today, we are grateful to Satguru Sivaya Subramuniyaswami for spreading the message to the modern society. In this respect, Gurudeva's recent addition, *Weaver's Wisdom*, an American English translation of *Tirukural*, is an additional tool that will be available to our people. This book will help us read and take in the essence of the teaching of our ancient poet Tiruvalluvar. The style adopted by Gurudeva is very simple and easy to read. The beautiful illustrations add more meaning and understanding to the reader. As I went over the different verses in *Weaver's Wisdom*, I came to realize that the most valuable achievement is leading a righteous life. I believe that reading the teachings in this holy book and applying them in our day-to-day activities will bring inner peace to us in today's stressful world. In conclusion, we will be failing in our duty if we do not attempt to teach *Weaver's Wisdom* to our children. This will enable them to live a disciplined life and to rise to the level of a perfect person, *sanroor*.

> **Dr. Shan A. Shanmugavadivel, Tamil Elder and Dental Practitioner; Toronto, Ontario, Canada**

I went through the book with tremendous interest. It is really a wonderful work and it shows Satguru Sivaya Subramuniyaswami's keen thought in promoting *Tirukural* to the West. I am sure it will be liked by people of all walks of life. An ancient Tamil once said, "To call anyone a poet upon this Earth besides the divine Tiruvalluvar would be like calling both the evening illumined by the moon and the evening shrouded in darkness a beautiful evening."

> **Dr. S. Sockalingam, M.B.B.S., M.C.G.P.; Klang, Malaysia**

Tirukural by the Tamil Saint Tiruvalluvar is a Tamil *Veda*, a book of divinity and high moral and spiritual values. It is such an ancient work as to influence the entire gamut of Tamil literature. Such an ancient treatise has been brought out in English by Satguru Swamiji as a divine gift to humanity. Satguru's compassion coupled with desire for welfare of the entire human race has inspired him to make this book available in an understandable language. ¶The author of this English version of *Tirukural*, Satguru Sivaya Subramuniyaswami, has taken great pains to explain the meaning and the sense of each verse in a lucid and easy style to enable everyone to understand the essence of the great sayings of Tiruvalluvar and to follow and practice them carefully in their day-to-day life. The translation is faithful to the original Tamil verses as also profound and precise. ¶The author's introduction to each section is informative, conveys the concept expounded in the section with conviction and clarity and talks briefly about the subject in the background of the vast experience of the author. ¶The Satguru's service in presenting this Tamil treatise in English is lofty and commendable and I am sure that the whole world will welcome this publication and will benefit by the profound knowledge contained in each *kural* verse.

Dr. P. Jayaraman, Executive Director, Bharatiya Vidya Bhavan, Institute of Indian Culture; New York, USA